"Heaven Is Like ..."

"Heaven Is Like …"

A Gospel Model for Writing, Preparing, and Delivering the Sunday Homily

Jay Cormier

SHEED & WARD
Franklin, Wisconsin

As an apostolate of the Priests of the Sacred Heart, a Catholic religious congregation, the mission of Sheed & Ward is to publish books of contemporary impact and enduring merit in Catholic Christian thought and action. The books published, however, reflect the opinions of their authors and are not meant to represent the official position of the Priests of the Sacred Heart.

2000

Sheed & Ward
7373 South Lovers Lane Road
Franklin, Wisconsin 53132
1-800-266-5564

Printed in the United States of America

Cover and interior design by Sheila von Driska

Cover art: "Christ Preaching," Rembrandt, public domain

Scripture quotations are from the New Revised Standard Version of the Bible, copyright 1989 by the Division of Christian Education of the National Council of the Churches of Christ in the USA. Used by permission. All rights reserved.

Excerpts from *Fulfilled in Your Hearing* copyright © 1982 United States Catholic Conference, Inc., Washington, D. C. Used with permission. All rights reserved. No part of this document may be reproduced by any means without permission in writing from the copyright owner.

Library of Congress Cataloging-in-Publication Data

Cormier, Jay.
    "Heaven is like" : a gospel model for writing, preparing, and delivering the Sunday homily by Jay Cormier.
        p.cm.
    ISBN 1-58051-072-8 (pbk. alk. paper)
    1. Preaching. 2. Storytelling—Religious aspects—Christianity.
3. Jesus Christ—Preaching. 4. Catholic preaching. I. Title.

BV4235.S76 C76 2000
251—dc21   99-056813
                                              CIP

1 2 3 4 5 / 03 02 01 00

For Ann

CONTENTS

INTRODUCTION

After the celebrant or deacon preaches the Sunday homily in our parish church, I can't help but wonder if he passed what I have come to think of as the "Kinnon test."

The Kinnons are one of the many wonderful families in our parish. Mom and Dad work three jobs between them to make a comfortable and loving home for their family. Their four children—ranging in age from seven to thirteen—are busy with school, their soccer games and sports schedules, and the many trials and tribulations of growing up. Their faith is very important to all of them—the family participates in the Eucharist every Sunday, two of the children are altar servers, another sings with the youth choir. Mom assists with the religious education program, and Dad helps out when he can on a number of parish programs.

As we begin the Profession of Faith, I always wonder if the homilist's words on this Sunday deepened any Kinnon's understanding of the depth of God's love for them. Was any Kinnon family member affirmed in the struggle to become a genuine disciple of Jesus? Were any members of the Kinnon clan challenged to be the salt and light of Christ in their Monday-through-Saturday worlds?

This book is about passing the "Kinnon test" each Sunday.

This book is about preaching as Jesus preached to the Kinnons and the McArdles and the O'Briens and the Milanos, and all the families that gathered around him along the Galilee shore and the Temple precincts.

This book is about helping these families realize the presence of God in their lives, about making God's love real to them in the midst of the storms that rock the small boats that are their lives.

This book is about developing and using the skills of speech communications to proclaim the good news of the resurrection in such a way that the community will embrace it with joy.

Just as Jesus did in all of his stories that began with "the kingdom of heaven is like . . ."

Many preachers, teachers, and communicators have contributed their wisdom, example, and inspiration to this book. I am and always will be grateful for their presence in my life. My thanks, too, to the many people whose stories and ideas appear here. A special word of appreciation to the deacons of New England and the bishops and priests of the Diocese of Scranton, Pennsylvania, for their gracious invitations to develop the ideas in this book in a series of workshops they asked me to lead. My thanks, too, to David Philippart of Liturgy Training Publications, who encouraged this project by publishing what has become chapter 1 in the April 1997 issue of *Liturgy 90*.

This author is most grateful to Keith McClellan, O.S.B. for his initial review of the manuscript, and for the work of Stephen Hrycyniak, Jeremy Langford, and Kass Dotterweich (who expertly edited the manuscript) of Sheed & Ward for shepherding this project from its original pile of scattered notes and ideas to the book you now hold in your hand. And it is due to the work of Tom Hoffman and his marketing staff at Sheed & Ward that you are holding this book at all.

No undertaking like this ever sees the light of day without the support, care, and more than a little patience from the writer's family and friends. This writer has been especially blessed in this regard. These few words do not begin to express the depth of love and gratitude to my wife and dearest friend, Ann.

A special note about the layout of the text. Many sample
homilies and story ideas appear throughout this book to illustrate the concepts explained in each chapter. In order to help
readers better capture the flow and rhythm of each sample sermon, these homilies have been broken down into "sense
lines"—each line concludes at a natural breaking or pause
point. The concept of writing in sense lines is explained in
greater detail in chapter 4.

May the approaches, ideas, and suggestions in the pages
that follow prove to be useful tools to you in your ministry of
preaching.

Chapter 1

A Gospel Model: "The Reign of God Is Like..."

Jesus told the crowds all these things in parables...
to fulfill what had been spoken through the prophet:
"I will open my mouth to speak in parables;
I will proclaim what has been hidden
from the foundation of the world."

Matthew 13: 34–35, Psalm 78:2

Many preachers and homilists construct their homilies each week like any public speaking assignment—an introduction, the development of three main points, and a conclusion. Sometimes they include—perhaps out of a sense of obligation (if this is going to be a "real" homily, after all)—some exegetical background on the three readings and an admonition to the congregation to either stop doing something or start doing something.

But consider for a moment not only Jesus' teachings, but his teaching *method* Jesus' words, especially his parables, are masterpieces of thoughtful, concise, and meaningful communication. The parable of the two sons (Matthew 21:28–32) is an example:

28 "A man had two sons;
    he went to the first and said,
    'Son, go and work in the vineyard today.'

29 He answered, 'I will not';
        but later he changed his mind and went.
30 The father went to the second and said the same;
        and he answered, 'I go, sir';
        but he did not go.
31 Which of the two did the will of his father?"
        [The chief priests and elders] said, "The first."
        Jesus said to them,
        "Truly I tell you,
        the tax collectors and the prostitutes
        are going into the kingdom of God ahead of you.
32 For John came to you in the way of righteousness
        and you did not believe him,
        but the tax collectors and the prostitutes
        believed him;
        and even after you saw it,
        you did not change your minds and believe him."

This parable, typical of Jesus' style of preaching, includes three elements:

- the *story* (or image) from the everyday world of his hearers. The story makes real for his listeners some truth about God's relationship with the human family, or reveals how God is present in the listeners' world—hidden, perhaps, but real nonetheless;

- the *connection* between that story and the reality of God's love—how the holy is present in the most unexpected of places;

- the *invitation* to embrace that love, to realize that presence in our lives.

All three elements are at work in the parable above.

- the *story* (28–31a): Every parent of every time and place knows all too well the struggle to get children to do their chores. Sometimes the request is met with whining, but eventually the chores get done. Sometimes, however, the child fails to transform the best of intentions into a completed task.

- the *connection* (31b–32a): Our response to God is often like that parent-child relationship: Some of us proudly claim to be God's own but do nothing to support that claim, while those of us who seem to be the antithesis of God's own may, in fact, be closer to God's way of holiness than those whose profession of faith is more conspicuous.

- the *invitation* (32b): Jesus concludes the parable by urging his hearers to embrace that same spirit of repentance and conversion.

Many other parables of Jesus are structured according to this *story/connection/invitation* model. Consider Matthew 25:31–46:

31 "When the Son of Man comes in his glory,
       and the angels with him,
       then he will sit on the throne of his glory.
32 All the nations will be gathered before him,
       and he will separate people one from another
       as a shepherd separates the sheep from the goats,
33 and he will put the sheep at his right hand
       and the goats at his left.
34 Then the king will say to those at his right hand,
       'Come, you that are blessed by my Father,
       inherit the kingdom prepared for you
       from the foundation of the world;

35 for I was hungry and you gave me food,
     I was thirsty and you gave me something to drink,
     I was a stranger and you welcomed me,
36 I was naked and you gave me clothing,
     I was sick and you took care of me,
     I was in prison and you visited me.'
37 Then the righteous will answer him,
     'Lord, when was it
     that we saw you hungry and gave you food,
     or thirsty and gave you something to drink?
38 And when was it
     that we saw you a stranger and welcomed you,
     or naked and gave you clothing?
39 And when was it
     that we saw you sick or in prison and visited you?'
40 And the king will answer them,
     'Truly I tell you,
     just as you did it to one of the least of these
     who are members of my family,
     you did it to me.'

41 "Then he will say to those at his left hand,
     'You that are accursed, depart from me
     into the eternal fire
     prepared for the devil and his angels;
42 for I was hungry and you gave me no food,
     I was thirsty and you gave me nothing to drink,
43 I was a stranger and you did not welcome me,
     naked and you did not give me clothing,
     sick and in prison and you did come to visit me.'
44 Then they also will answer,
     'Lord, when was it
     that we saw you hungry or thirsty
     or a stranger or naked or sick or in prison,
     and did not take care of you?'

45 Then he will answer them,
      'Truly I tell you,
      just as you did not do it
      to one of the least of these,
      you did not do it to me.'
46 And these will go away into eternal punishment,
      but the righteous into eternal life."

In verse 32 of this, his last parable before the events of his passion unfold, Jesus depicts the final judgment of humankind as "a shepherd separates the sheep from the goats" (*story*). The "sheep" are welcomed into the kingdom of God for their faithfulness in embracing the shepherd's spirit of selfless service to others; the "goats," however, are condemned for their failure to recognize the humble Son of Man in those who come to them in need (*connection*). The sheep's reward and the goats' condemnation are an *invitation* to every would-be disciple to see the face of Christ the servant in the face of the poor, the needy, and the troubled: ". . . just as you did it to one of the least of these who are members of my family, you did it to me" (40).

In another parable (Luke 16:1–8), Jesus astonishes his listeners by his admiration for the corrupt manager who holds on to his job by cooking the books:

1 "There was a rich man who had a manager,
      and charges were brought to him
      that this man was squandering his property.
2 So he summoned him and said to him,
      'What is this that I hear about you?
      Give me an accounting of your management,
      because you cannot be my manager any longer.'
3 Then the manager said to himself,
      'What will I do,
      now that my master is taking the position
      away from me?
      I am not strong enough to dig,

and I am ashamed to beg.
4 I have decided what to do so that,
   when I am dismissed as manager,
   people may welcome me into their homes.'

5 So, summoning his master's debtors one by one,
   he asked the first,
   'How much do you owe my master?'
6 He answered, 'A hundred jugs of olive oil.'
   He said to him,
   'Take your bill, sit down quickly, and make it fifty.'
7 Then he asked another,
   'And how much do you owe?'
   He replied, 'A hundred containers of wheat.'
   He said to him,
   'Take your bill and make it eighty.'

8 And his master commended the dishonest manager
   because he had acted shrewdly;
   for the children of this age are more shrewd
   in dealing with their own generation
   than are the children of light."

Jesus, of course, is not advising his followers to engage in fraud; rather, Jesus seeks to impress upon us how ready we are to employ all our initiative and ingenuity in acquiring material wealth (*connection*). Should we not be, Jesus asks, as enterprising and resourceful—and dedicated—to the lasting things of God as we are to the fleeting things of the world (*invitation*)?

Now, one could argue quite correctly that this approach easily "fits" the standard speech-class model of introduction/three points/conclusion. But the *story/connection/invitation* model, by taking such a specific approach to structuring the message, makes critical demands of homilists in their preparation and writing of a homily. Approaching the homily using this model can help many homilists think through and deliver—and, consequently, communicate—a more effective, meaningful homily to their worshiping communities.

Finding the Extraordinary in the Ordinary

The genius of Jesus' parables is their ability to take the ordinary and, through them, reveal the *extra*ordinary. Through stories about wayward children, lost coins, unexpected discoveries, paychecks, mustard seeds, and weeds, Jesus makes the presence of God real in the lives of his hearers.

Teachers and experts in homiletics have said that storytelling is the most effective form of preaching. While most homilists know this is true, many shy away from the role of "storyteller," fearing that they lack the necessary acting skills and personality to keep an audience enthralled with a tale of any consequence. But storytelling does not necessarily mean long and detailed narratives with intricate plots and a full cast of characters. Good stories can be simple images and word-pictures that people know and see and feel. One of the foremost storytellers of our time, Garrison Keillor, says that a good story "allows people to come into it. You can somehow envision yourself as a participant in a story."[1]

Sometimes a homily's story will have all of the dramatic elements of plot, confrontation, climax, and resolution, or the comic setup and the well-timed punch line; often, however, a picture painted in words or the relating of a situation or experience common to everyone becomes a story that tells itself in the imagination of the listener. These simple "stories" can reveal a faith that is just as real and meaningful as the most cleverly developed yarn. With the right image suggested by the homilist, listeners can tell their own stories.

Several years ago, when the concept of preaching a homily at every Sunday Eucharist was still a novel concept in many parishes, the U.S. Catholic Bishops' Committee on Priestly Life and Ministry published a reflection on the restored place of the homily in the Liturgy of the Word. *Fulfilled in Your Hearing* includes this insightful definition:

> The role of the homilist is to help people *make the connections* between the reality of their lives and the reality of the Gospel . . . to help them see how God in Jesus Christ has entered and identified himself with the human realities of pain and happiness (emphasis added).

How succinctly and accurately put. This communication, which is an act of both liturgical prayer and ministry, should make Sunday's Gospel real to the Monday-through-Saturday world of the parish community. Among the implications for the homilist, then, is the need to be in touch with that world. This is the ministerial dimension of homiletics: to love one's community enough to listen to them, to travel with them on their journeys, to honor their struggles to live faithfully in a world working overtime to sterilize itself of God's presence.

Sadly, too many homilies today are long on admonition and condemnation but short on invitation. Invitation is an act between equals. It is not arrogant, belittling, or self-righteous. It is not satisfied with simply pointing to evil in our midst; rather, it takes on the harder, more challenging work of pointing to the good in the midst of evil. Invitation does not wallow in the stridency and anger of Jeremiah ("Woe to you, Jerusalem"; Jeremiah 13:27) but finds reason to hope in the joy of Andrew ("Come and see the Lord"; John 1:41). Invitation is not the demand of a self-appointed expert or professional who believes he/she is the proprietor of some special insight to be given to lesser lights, but a humble welcoming into the vineyard by a brother/sister pilgrim.

Which is *not* to say that invitation cannot or should not be admonition. The concept of invitation does not water down the message but confronts the truth with honesty and integrity. Invitation does not limit itself to the easy route of pointing to evil but takes on the harder, more challenging task of pointing to the good in the midst of that evil. Invitation does not deny the cross but embraces it with Easter hope.

Simply put, the invitation dimension of the homily never abandons the community at the hopelessness of Calvary but always brings the community to the joy of Easter's empty tomb.

Homily #1: Michelangelo in our midst

The *story/connection/invitation* model was put to use by one homilist on the Solemnity of the Lord's Ascension. In reflecting on the readings, the homilist was struck by Jesus' call to his disciples of every age to be his "witnesses . . . to the ends of the earth" (Acts 1:8). Such "witness" often comes at a price.

In the spring of 1996, news media across the country carried the story of the discovery of an authentic Michelangelo sculpture in a New York mansion. The preacher of the following homily had read the story of Professor Kathleen Weil-Garris Brandt's painstaking and professionally risky work to prove that the statue of Cupid was, indeed, the work of the great artist. The homilist saw in the story a parallel to the hard and demanding role of being an authentic witnesses to the risen Christ.

The homilist began by telling the community the *story*, retold from articles in *The New York Times* and *Newsweek*:

The three-foot-high statue of Cupid
had stood in the entrance of the New York mansion
for almost a century.
Nobody paid much attention to the nondescript sculpture,
covered with cracks and stains,
its arms broken off long ago,
its nose and upper lip badly chipped.

The mansion currently houses
the French embassy's cultural mission.
One night last October,
the mansion was brilliantly lighted
for the opening of an exhibition of French decorative arts.

That night, Professor Kathleen Weil-Garris Brandt
passed the mansion on her way home
from her office and classes
at New York University's Institute of Fine Arts.
On a whim, she decided to walk up the steps
and press her nose against the glass door to sneak a peak.

There, under the bright lights of the reception,
she saw something that made her heart race.
She recognized the little statue
in the center of the entry.
She was positive she had seen it in a 1902 catalog
identifying it as one of the rarest of art works:
a genuine Michelangelo.

Now, such claims, if not well founded,
can be professional suicide in the art world.
Professor Brandt—
who also serves as a consultant to the Vatican Museums—
proceeded cautiously.
With the permission of the French cultural attaché,
she began a detailed study of the statue—
and became convinced that it was the real thing.

"It looked like the work of a teenage Michelangelo,"
she concluded,
pointing to a number of the artist's distinctive techniques,
such as Cupid's quiver in the shape of a lion's paw,
the forms and features of the face,
and the flickering curls of the hair.

The world's leading Renaissance scholars
have reviewed her studies and concur with her findings—
that the little statue is the work the great Michelangelo.

One noted Renaissance scholar had especially high praise
for Professor Brandt's careful work:
"You are not going to make any discoveries in this field,"
the scholar wrote,
"unless you have the nerve to commit yourself,
the courage to entertain the idea
that it might be by Michelangelo,
and eventually to say that you think it is by him."

Next, the homilist forged the link between the *story* and
the theme of the Ascension Gospel—the "*connection* between
the reality of [the hearers'] lives and the reality of the Gospel":

In her courage to imagine the possibilities,
in her dedication to seek out the truth,
in her love and passion for her profession,
Professor Brandt discovered an extraordinary treasure—
a treasure that, for decades,
art historians have hobnobbed within touching distance of,
but never realized.

On the Mount of the Ascension,
Jesus calls his disciples
to be his "witnesses to the ends of the earth."
Such "witness" demands the same dedication to truth,
the same love and passion,
and often the same risk
as Professor Brandt took in her work.
To be "witnesses" of the Risen One demands a dedication
to seeking out what is good, right, and just.

To be "witnesses" of the Risen One
is to recognize his presence not just in this holy place
but in our homes, schools, and workplaces—
thus making them "holy places" as well.

To be "witnesses" of the Risen One
is to possess the courage
to endure ridicule and misunderstanding
and to risk our own safety and comfort
for the sake of that gospel.
But in dedicating ourselves to being Christ's "witnesses,"
we uncover a great treasure that is forgotten
but never lost:
the love, hope, and compassion of God.

The homilist then concluded with an *invitation*, beautifully expressed by the apostle Paul in the second reading for Ascension Thursday (Ephesians 1:17–23):

As Paul writes to the Ephesians in today's second reading,
"with a spirit of wisdom and insight to know him clearly"
and an "innermost vision [to] know
the great hope to which he has called [us],"
may we have the courage, perseverance, and commitment
to uncover the great treasure in our midst—
the Easter Christ.

Homily #2: First plantings

A homilist can sometimes simply suggest an idea or paint a picture in words that will lead the community to imagine their own "stories." Within their own imaginations, the hearers will "enter" (to use Garrison Keillor's definition of story) their own story, considering what they would do or how they would respond to the "story" that the homilist suggests.

Preaching on the parable of the mustard seed (Matthew 13:31–32), a homilist began by asking the community:

Remember learning to read in the first grade?
It probably began with a series of cards or posters:
A is for apple,
B is for ball,
C is for cookie,
D is for dog.
And we would work so hard to learn those sounds:
aa-pple,
b-all,
k-ookie,
d-og.
Once we learned to attach the right sound to its letter,
we were able to identify groups of letters
that formed words.
And once we were able to "sound out" words,
we were able to enter the incredible world of reading—
a whole new world of books and magazines and plays.
Think how far you've come
since "See John run" was the height of great literature.

And then there were numbers.
First we had to recognize that the numerals 1 through 10
represented specific amounts of apples, cookies, pennies.
Then we moved on,
with the help of apple-pie tins,
to fractions.
The next time you struggle balancing your checkbook
or marvel at the power of your laptop computer,
remember that it all began with ten apples.

Remember the first time you met your spouse?
Maybe it was a chance meeting with a simple "Hello";
a few awkward words might have been exchanged.

Then you screwed up your courage
to ask her out on your first real date,
and somehow, you connected—
a relationship began and love blossomed.
But it all began with that simple "Hello,"
with a few awkward words.

Each one of these short word-pictures triggered *stories* and memories for everyone in the congregation. The homilist then *connected* the stories he prompted to the Gospel theme of the importance of small things in our lives.

All of the great events and moments of life
begin with small things—
every great novel is written with the same twenty-six letters;
every magnificent symphony is composed
    on the same musical scale;
every critical formula is a combination
    of the numbers we learned in first grade;
every great love story begins
    with a few awkward words of conversation.
From basic elements and fundamental ideas
life's greatest accomplishments are born,
life's most exciting journeys begin.

Jesus' parable of the mustard seed challenges us
to create the kingdom of God here, among us,
    in the same way:
humanity's dreams of peace, community, and justice
will be realized, first,
in the simple, basic, and unseen acts of such goodness
    by individual men and women.
Such is "mustard seed" faith:
that, from the smallest and humblest acts
    of justice, kindness, and compassion,
the kingdom of God will grow.

Peace in the world must begin with peace in our homes.
People and nations will be reconciled
only when we cherish reconciliation and forgiveness
within our own families and among our own friends.
The justice of God will transform
the major issues of our day
only when those same principles of justice and mercy
take root in our own decision making,
in our own standards of morality and ethics,
in our own approach to what is right and wrong.

The homilist concluded by *inviting* his hearers to embrace "mustard seed" faith.

"Mustard seed faith" is not always easy—
we tend to demand solutions to big problems immediately;
we have little patience for the small and simple,
convinced, instead, that bigger is better
and the more complex, the more effective.
But Jesus asks us to approach life
with the simple faith of the mustard seed:
that from the smallest act of goodness,
from the most hidden offer of mercy and forgiveness,
from the most personal conviction of right
    in the face of doubt and ridicule,
a mighty tree will take root,
an abundant harvest will be realized.

Homily #3: The hard work of hate

God is at work in every story. If one knows where to look—and how to look with the eyes of faith—the love of God is found in stories of joy and sorrow, stories of victories and tragedies, in stories that provoke tears and stories that provoke laughter.

Lynn Johnston's daily newspaper comic strip *For Better or For Worse* chronicles the daily adventures of the Patterson family. The day-to-day trials and tribulations encountered by the Pattersons—Mom Ellie, Dad John, college student son Michael, teenage daughter Elizabeth (Lizzy), and eight-year-old daughter April—mirror the stories encountered by every family in the challenging, complex world we live in.

In one episode, Lizzy discovers not only what a sad and destructive emotion hate is but how demanding hating someone can be. One homilist found Elizabeth's experience a good starting point (*story*) for a reflection on Jesus' preaching about loving only those who love us (Matthew 5:43–48):

In Lynn Johnson's wonderful daily comic strip
about the simple joys and travails of family life,
For Better or For Worse,
teenager Lizzy has had a fight with her friend Candace
     over a boy.
The two are not speaking.
In the first panel,
Lizzy and Candace walk right by each other.
"There's Candace," Lizzy says to herself,
"I do not know her."

Second panel, in the corridor, on the way to class:
"She's going down the hall one way,
so I'll go the other way.
If she sits near me in class, I'll move!!"

Third panel, in class:
"Here comes Candace.
If she talks to me, I'll pretend I didn't hear her.
If she looks at me, I'll pretend I didn't see her."

In the final panel,
with Candace sitting in the background,

Lizzy puts her head in her hands and realizes,
"Whew! I didn't think hating somebody
   could be so much WORK!" [2]

The homilist then made the *connection* between Lizzy's discovery and Jesus' Sermon on the Mount:

It's true, isn't it?
To really *hate* someone
demands a great deal of wasted time, energy, and emotion.
But God's gift of life is not meant to be squandered
on estrangement and alienation
but to be celebrated in the love of family and friends.

The challenge of the Gospel is to be ready and willing
to take that first difficult step
   toward forgiving and seeking forgiveness;
to refuse to allow bitterness to close our hearts to someone,
   regardless of how deeply they hurt us;
to put aside our own need for the justice "due" us
   for the good of others.

The homilist then *invited* the community to embrace such a change of heart and perspective:

As Lizzy discovers with Candace
—and as we all know,
even though we are reluctant to admit it—
this life God has given each one of us
is too precious, too short,
to waste on anything less than the love of God, its Giver.
We all know someone from whom we are estranged,
individuals we can't stand,
people we would rather have nothing to do with.
Isn't there an avenue we can take,
an opening we can explore,

a hand we can extend
to heal wounds
and mend bridges between us and them?
Not to do so is such a waste of time and energy.
After all, there are so many better things to do
than to waste time and energy on *hating*.
It's too much work.

The *story/connection/invitation* model requires homilists to keep their antennae up and feelers out for the unmistakable signs of God's presence in the world they share with their worshiping community. Sometimes, the Gospel reading will trigger a story; at other times, a story, an event, or an image will come first, opening up in the homilist's imagination a new dimension to a particular Gospel theme. To preach as Jesus preached is, first and always, a matter of being in touch with the Word—the Word of God both made flesh in Jesus and fleshed out in the people of God and the world God gave them.

And that is what transforms preaching from a last-minute Saturday morning stressed-filled burden into a week-long ministry of service, in imitation of the preacher Jesus, who "opened [his] mouth in parables . . . to proclaim what had been hidden from the foundation of the world."

The next chapter will look at the different kinds of stories and how to tell them. Chapter 3 will focus on how to make the connection between the reality of God's love and the reality of the everyday human experience, between our stories and the story of God. Chapter 4 discusses an "inviting" style of preaching, and Chapter 5 offers a number of practical suggestions and insights from renowned preachers and professional communicators for homilists on their "journey" to Sunday.

Chapter 2

Story:
To "Reveal
What Is Hidden"

The reign of God is like
>*a farmer who sowed good seed in his field . . .*
>*a mustard seed . . .*
>*the yeast a woman used to make bread . . .*
>*a treasure hidden in a field . . .*
>*a dragnet cast into the sea . . .*
>*a king who decided to settle accounts . . .*
>*the owner of a vineyard . . .*
>*ten bridesmaids who took their lamps and went out
> to meet the groom . . .*
>*a man who entrusted property to his servants . . .*
>*a fig tree . . .*

Throughout the Gospels, Jesus spoke not in the abstract theological concepts of the learned Pharisee but in the simple eloquence of his hearers' everyday experience. The most profound dimensions of Christ's teachings were made clear to the gruff shepherd, the peasant woman, and the simple child through stories about wayward children, unscrupulous servants, poor beggars, lost coins, and mustard seeds. Jesus' listeners were able to grasp in his stories the meaning of the deepest mysteries of faith: God as Creator and Father of all humankind, the dawning of God's mercy in the coming of the Messiah, the joys of simple charity.

Storytelling is the most effective form of communication. Great ideas and concepts can be envisioned and embraced through narrative. But stories do not have to include the dramatic elements of plot, complication, climax, and denouement to be effective. A single image or picture that listeners recognize, see, and feel can be a powerful story in itself. As Garrison Keillor observed, what makes a good story is its ability to invite people "into" it—listeners find themselves wondering what they would do in this story, how they would cope with the conflict or issue, how they would interact with the characters. The right image or idea can trigger the listeners' own stories relived on the stages of their memories and imagination. From such stories a homilist can share faith that is meaningful and real.

Consider the following *story* told by a homilist preaching on Jesus' words on treasuring the things of God before all else (Matthew 6:24–34):

He got the idea that Sunday
when they went to their son's for dinner.
They spent a wonderful afternoon
with their beloved granddaughter—
including a tea party in her playroom
with all her favorite dolls invited.

That's when he got the idea for the dollhouse.

He started drawing up plans that same night.
In the middle of a critical business meeting,
an idea would strike him
and he would start sketching it on his pad—
while a vice president droned on
about cost overruns for a new downtown office tower,
he would be roughing in a new porch for the dollhouse.

Over the years, he had built up
one of the region's largest construction companies.

He oversaw millions of dollars of construction projects—
schools, office buildings, condominiums.
But at the top of his packed brief case
and always in the front of his mind
was the dollhouse.

Every evening, after a long day at his office,
he would adjourn to his basement workshop.
Carefully he worked each piece of wood—
cutting, sanding, planing, fitting, gluing, painting.
Oh, he could have had his own architects and carpenters
construct a beautiful dollhouse in a matter of hours.
But he never considered that.
This project was his from start to finish.
After all, it was for a very special client.

When he presented the dollhouse to his granddaughter
and gave her the grand tour
of its meticulously crafted rooms and furnishings,
the little girl was speechless;
she glowed with that look of wonder and joy
that only a child possesses.
She put her small arms around his neck and said,
"Thank you, Grandpa! Thank you!
I love my dollhouse!
And I love you!"

That was almost five years ago.
The dollhouse is still cherished by his granddaughter,
who will, one day, give the house to her little girl.

If you ask him
what building he's proudest of in his long career,
he won't even mention the university library
or the downtown church or the modern office tower.

Instead, he'll smile
and tell you about this incredible dollhouse he crafted
for one very special client.

This story is simply a word-picture. We can see Grandpa planning each stage of the dollhouse. We can imagine him scribbling on his pad during one of those tedious meetings many of us have suffered through ourselves. We know the love that generates such enthusiasm for a project like this, and we have seen the delight in the face of a child who receives such a special gift.

The homilist used this word-picture to make the point that faith calls us to treasure the important things of life—like the love of those who are most important to us—and to remind us that we are called to embrace the values and spirit not of life's passing stages but of dollhouses handcrafted for a granddaughter's birthday.

A good story, too, can simply suggest a situation or set of circumstances that triggers the listener's own story. A homilist did exactly that when he asked his community on the First Sunday of Advent:

Have you ever fallen asleep while driving?
It's a horrifying realization.
But it happens to all of us.
The rain,
the rhythm of the windshield wipers,
the endless miles of white highway lines
can lull you to sleep without your realizing it.
Then, all of a sudden,
you are startled by an oncoming car's headlights
or a blasting truck horn
and you discover that your car
is veering into the opposite lane
and heading for a guardrail or embankment.

Instantly you steer your car
back into the center of your lane.

The rest of your trip is not the same.
If you're smart,
you'll pull over, stop, and give yourself a break.
The importance of wherever you are going
     diminishes considerably.
When you start out again,
you're prepared with gum to chew,
coffee to drink,
and music to play on the radio or tape deck or CD player.
You have a new, sobering awareness
of the need to stay awake.

Many of us, if we have not actually found ourselves falling asleep at the wheel of a car, certainly have been terrified by the possibility. From that image, the homilist developed the Advent call to stay awake, to be on constant watch for the coming of our God.

Stories can take different forms and be found in different places and contexts. There is the Gospel story "re-cast"; stories of "words made flesh"; parables of other places and times; stories of God's Spirit alive in our world; stories of saints and prophets among us; stories of the human dimension of God's Word; stories about "small" moments of grace within larger stories; stories about finding the extraordinary in the ordinary; and stories that provide us "a time to laugh."

The Gospel Story "Re-cast"

The stories and events recorded in the four Gospels speak of universal truths. The imaginative homilist can sometimes effectively "re-cast" a Gospel parable in a contemporary setting, enhancing its impact on today's hearer. This first story is

an example of a contemporary retelling of the parable of the
sheep and the goats (Matthew 25:31–46):

And when the Son of Man comes in glory,
escorted by the angels of heaven,
he will take his place upon his royal throne,
and all the peoples of every nation
will be assembled before him.

He will separate them into two groups,
as a shepherd separates sheep from goats.

To the sheep on his right, he will say:

"Come, you have inherited my Father's blessing!
For when a soup kitchen opened in your town,
    you volunteered to help.
When a group home for the mentally handicapped
    was opened in your neighborhood,
    you welcomed them.
When workers were subjected
    to unhealthy working conditions and unjust wages,
    you held their employers accountable.
When efforts were made
    to provide health care for all people,
    you thought first of the family who lost their home
    because of a catastrophic illness
    before you thought of your own pocketbook.

"For when you reached out to help
the homeless mother and her children,
the hungry vagrant at the soup kitchen,
the mentally handicapped neighbor,
the abused laborer,
the unemployed husband desperately trying to find

medical care for his dying wife,
you reached out to me."

But to those on his left, the Son of Man will say:

"Out of my sight, you condemned!
For when a soup kitchen opened in your town,
    you demanded that the police drive away
    those crazy, dangerous vagrants.
When a group home for the mentally handicapped
    was opened in your neighborhood,
    you cried, 'Not in *my* backyard!'
When workers were subjected
    to unhealthy working conditions and unjust wages,
    you dismissed their plight
    as the cost of doing business.
When efforts were made
    to provide health care for all people,
    you demanded to know why you should have to pay
    for someone else's problems.

"For when you rejected
the homeless mother and her children,
the hungry vagrant at the soup kitchen,
the mentally handicapped neighbor,
the abused laborer,
the unemployed husband desperately trying to find
    medical care for his dying wife,
you rejected me."

An imaginative preacher gives us a second example in this
re-casting of the parable of the Pharisee and the tax collector
(Luke 18:9–14) into a contemporary context that provides a
new insight into Jesus' invitation to embrace his spirit of humble servanthood:

The priest takes a chair near the altar.
He opens his prayer book and,
for the next twenty minutes or so,
praises God with the music of the psalmist.
As he closes the book at the end of "his" office,
the needs of his people come rushing
    into his mind and heart:

"Lord, how can we invigorate this parish?
How do we get people excited about the RCIA,
about our Lenten lecture series,
about our family enrichment programs?
How do we make parents realize their responsibility
in the religious education of their kids?
Why are our Sunday numbers down?
We're starting to feel it in the collection.
Lord, why don't people care about you anymore?"

Lost in his prayer,
the priest does not notice
the woman slipping through the back door
    of the church.
She has just dropped off one son to soccer practice
and a daughter to her piano lesson.
The car is filled with next week's groceries
while this week's laundry awaits at home.
The demands of the office fill her days;
the needs of her family fill her evenings.
These few minutes are very precious to her.
She quietly slumps in the last pew.
Her prayer consists only of,
"Lord, it's me, Margaret.
Help me get through it all."

In our own time and place,
the parable of the Pharisee and the tax collector
is played out

not so much as a lack of humility
but as a lack of awareness of the needs,
the hopes,
the cries of help of those around us.
In our busyness to get things done for others,
we begin to see them as objects of charity
rather than as our brothers and sisters
who deserve our help
only because they, like us,
are children of God.

Humility before God demands
humility before others,
seeing them as God sees us,
loving them as God loves us.

Finally, a re-casting that breathes fresh meaning into one of
Jesus' most beautiful parables:

The executive has been working late at the office.
Around 11:00,
he leaves the building
and proceeds across the brightly lit street
to his car in the dark parking lot.

Just as he senses that he is not alone,
he is pushed to the ground.
He is beaten, kicked,
stripped of his watch,
his ring, his wallet, his brief case.
People across the street hear some commotion,
but they keep walking:
Whatever it is, the police will take care of it.

A street person is wandering through the parking lot.
He has spent another day

panhandling for nickels, dimes, and quarters
at bus stops, street corners, and subway stations.
He is the kind we instinctively avoid—
the "odor" of his presence arrives
several seconds before he does.
The vagrant stumbles over the man who has been mugged.
He helps the semi-conscious, bleeding executive
     to his feet,
gathers up what's left of the man's possessions—
he finds the brief case a few yards away
and picks up as many of the papers and notes as he can find.

He then takes the man by the arm
and leads him across the street
to where he knows there is a bank of pay phones.
He then reaches into his dirty, tattered pockets,
pulls out his last few coins,
and gives them to the man to call home.

So who was neighbor to the man who was mugged?

Note that most of these stories are told by the homilist in
the present tense rather than the past. Employing the present
tense in narrative gives the story a sense of immediacy that
helps listeners reconstruct each element of the story in their
own minds as it is being told. By telling these stories as if they
are unfolding now, before our mind's eye, the stories become
living realities in the listeners' imaginations.

Stories of "Words Made Flesh"

Throughout the Gospels, certain sayings of Jesus seem to echo
within our consciousness. The words may strike an urgent truth
("It will not be so among you"; Matthew 20:26) or provide a
new way of looking at the human condition ("but, I tell you,

seventy-seven times"; Matthew 18:22) or touch us with particular poignancy ("Father, forgive them; for they do not know what they are doing"; Luke 23:34).

One homilist was particularly struck by the question Jesus asks his disciples at Caesari Philippi (Matthew 16:13–20):

When you want to strike back at your spouse
with a sharp word—or worse,
Who do you say I am?

When you're about to join in the taunting
of one of those geeky, nerdy kids at school,
Who do you say I am?

When that obnoxious, stupid, self-righteous,
perpetually complaining bore in the office
has pushed you to the edge,
Who do you say I am?

When your son or daughter needs help
with that school project
but the newspaper remains to be read
or tee time is approaching,
Who do you say I am?

When yet another appeal is made
on your time or your wallet
on behalf of the sick, the poor, or the troubled,
Who do you say I am?

The question Jesus asks Peter and the disciples
is asked of each of us every minute of every day.
Every decision we make is ultimately
a response to the question,
Who do you say I am?

[Notice, too, the impact made by repeating the words of Jesus—*Who do you say I am?*—after each story.]

Good storytellers are able to get inside the head of a character and convey to listeners exactly what makes that character tick. One homilist suggested this insightful portrait of the rich young man who seeks to enter Jesus' company (Mark 10:17–30):

So the rich young man asked Jesus:
"What must I do to share in everlasting life?"
Jesus looked at the young man with love and said,
"Go and sell what you have
and give it to the poor;
you will then have treasure in heaven."
The young man went away sad,
for he had many possessions.

"I knew it," he said to himself,
"another bleeding heart do-gooder.
'Sell what you have and give it to the poor.'
Sure. Easy for him. He has nothing.
It's always the same spiel.
I thought this Jesus was different.
Give all you got.
Like it's going to make a difference.
If I sell everything,
I might make a few people less poor,
but it won't have any real impact on the system.
Help the poor by becoming poor?
Typical liberal approach.
Having treasure in heaven is fine,
but what about making it through this hell on earth?
Being poor is better than being rich?
Trust me:
Being poor is not all it's cracked up to be.
Who pays the taxes that support welfare programs?
Who pays the wages to workers

so they can feed their families?
Who supports the temples and schools and academies?

'Sell what you have and give it to the poor'?
Try again, Jesus.
This rabbi is just another one of those
     traveling religious medicine shows.

Oh, he talks a great line.
But he just doesn't understand the way life is.
This Jesus just doesn't get it."

The homilist went on to suggest that the rich young man exists in many of us. Listen very carefully to what Jesus says in this Gospel: He does not condemn wealth and possessions as evil in themselves; rather, what *is* evil is the pursuit of wealth displacing God as the center of our lives. Given the choice between the life of God and the life of consumerism, the young man chooses consumerism. It's the young man who "just doesn't get it."

In the following homily, the preacher imagines how today's busy business managers, professionals, parents, and students might react to Jesus' instructions to the seventy-two disciples he commissions and sends off ahead of him in pairs to every town and place he himself intended to visit (Luke 10:1–12, 17–20):

In sending out the seventy-two,
Jesus insists that they travel light:
"Do not take a travel bag with you."
Is Jesus kidding?!
Our lives revolve around the contents
     of our travel bags—
our brief cases, attaches, book bags,
     purses, tote bags, luggage, shoulder bags.
Why, we couldn't survive

without the papers, books, notes, memoranda,
calculators, cameras, pills, cosmetics, cigarettes,
and whatever else we have stuffed inside!

And leave behind my calendar book?
My calendar book *is* my life!
Lose my calendar book and my life is,
for all intents and purposes,
OVER!

Leave behind my travel bag?
Jesus, you might as well ask me to leave behind my *life*.

That's exactly what I'm asking you to do,
Jesus would respond.
Unpack the things that clutter your life
in order to make room for the things of God.
Leave behind those things—and values—
that overwhelm your life
with the mindless pursuit of wealth, status, and power,
and pursue instead love, mercy, justice, peace.
Throw away that calendar that rules your time
and take possession of your life
as a gift from God
for the things of God.

Oh, it's easier said then done, of course,
but clearing out the clutter of our lives
in order to make room in our spirits and consciences
for the more important values of God
is a constant struggle for the faithful disciple.

We have been called by Jesus to focus our lives
not on the boxes of stuff we accumulate
but on the treasures of God that we carry
within our hearts and spirits.

Parables of Other Places and Times

Every people and culture of every age develop a tradition of stories, myths, and folktales. These stories help a people understand its identity and history, and illuminate the truths in which their values and sense of morality are grounded. Many of these parables and fables can open new and meaningful understandings of the ways of God as well.

The following story, recounted by Rabbi Harold S. Kushner in his best-selling *When Bad Things Happen to Good People*, challenges all of us to take on the work of becoming messengers of God's compassion, justice, and peace:

> There is an old Chinese tale
> about a woman whose only son died.
> In her grief,
> she pleaded with a monk renowned for his holiness:
> "What prayers, what magical incantations do you have
> to bring my son back to life?"
> Instead of sending her away or trying to reason with her,
> the monk said,
> "Fetch me a mustard seed
> from a home that has never known sorrow.
> We will use it to drive the sorrow out of your life."
>
> The woman set off at once
> in search of such a magical mustard seed.
>
> She came first to a splendid mansion,
> knocked at the door, and said,
> "I am looking for a home that has never known sorrow.
> Is this such a place?
> It is very important to me."
> They told her,
> "You've certainly come to the wrong place,"
> and then began to describe the tragic things

that had befallen their household.
The woman said to herself,
Who is better able to help these poor unfortunate people
than I who have had misfortune of my own?
She stayed to comfort them,
then went on in her search
for a home that had never known sorrow.

But wherever she stopped,
in hovels and palaces,
she found one tale after another
of sadness and misfortune.
Ultimately, she became so involved
in ministering to other people's grief
that she forgot her quest for the magical mustard seed,
never realizing that it had, in fact,
driven the sorrow out of her life.[1]

There are many insightful tales from American letters as well. The following is a retelling of Nathaniel Hawthorne's short story *The Minister's Black Veil:*

Many years ago,
the congregation of a small New England church
was stunned one Sunday morning
when their respected young minister,
the Reverend Mr. Hooper,
entered the church
wearing a veil of black crepe over his face.
The veil had a chilling effect on the congregation.
The minister conducted the service as usual,
with no reference to the veil—
but its very presence evoked much fear,
anxiety, mistrust, and wild speculation among parishioners.

A deputation confronted the Reverend Mr. Hooper
    about the veil
and his reasons for continuing to wear it.
The minister answered simply,
"If I hide my face for sorrow,
there is cause enough,
but if I cover it for secret sin,
what mortal might not do the same?"

And for the rest of his long life,
"Father" Hooper refused to take off the veil.
His congregation eventually came to accept the veil
and their esteem for his ministry grew.
But even on his death bed,
when an attending minister tried to remove it,
the elderly minister,
though sick and confused,
clutched the veil tightly to his face.

"Why do you tremble at me alone?" he cried.
"Tremble also at each other!
Have men avoided me,
and women shown no pity,
and children screamed and fled,
only for my black veil . . . ?
I look around me, and lo!
on every visage do I see a Black Veil!"

One homilist shared Hawthorne's story with his congregation in connection with the Lenten Gospel of Jesus' raising his
friend Lazarus from the dead (John 11:1–44). In the light of
that Gospel story, Hawthorne's dark fable is transformed into
one of hope: As the wrappings and "veil" of the dead are
removed from the entombed Lazarus, the risen Christ removes
those "veils" of fear, mistrust, prejudice, and ignorance with

which we bind and hide ourselves—like the black veil with which the Reverend Mr. Hooper shrouds himself.

Stories of God's Spirit Alive in our World

God is present in every event of human history; God's hand can be found touching every who/what/where/when/why/how of every day's headlines.

The Spirit of God was clearly at work, for example, in the wake of the tragic Oklahoma City bombing in June 1995:

What happened in Oklahoma City
is impossible to understand.
How any human beings could be so filled with hate,
so twisted by evil,
so mired in rage
that they could kill and maim
so many innocent men, women, and children
is incomprehensible.

And yet, amid the horror are tales of heroism.
Within seconds of the blast,
medical and emergency professionals and volunteers
rushed to the scene
to help rescue the injured buried under the rubble
of what was once the Alfred P. Murrah Federal Building.
Thousands of doctors, nurses, medical students,
police, firefighters, clergy, engineers, and blood donors
came to offer whatever help and expertise they could.

Medical professionals and rescue teams
not only from Oklahoma
but from surrounding states came as well.

Within hours,
church and social service agencies across the country

mobilized their networks of volunteers
to provide donations of food, clothing, and equipment.

Rescue teams worked day and night,
many refusing to leave at the end of their shifts.
They clawed through the rubble with axes and crowbars,
an inch at a time.
Rescuers were ordered to visit counselors
for help in coping with what they were seeing,
but many wanted only to get back inside the building
while there was still any hope at all
that someone might still be alive
under the twisted steel and shattered concrete.
While the building's shell shook and teetered dangerously,
doctors, nurses, and firefighters risked their own lives
crawling into airless cracks
to treat someone found still alive—
in fact, one nurse, Rebecca Anderson,
died as a result of injuries sustained
when she was hit by a piece of falling debris.
Despite the rash of bomb threats
that followed the explosion,
many nurses refused to leave their patients
when ordered to do so.

People waited in line for six hours
to donate blood at the Red Cross.
A sporting goods store
shipped every single one of its stock of knee pads
    to rescuers scouring the wreckage.
Churches served as relief centers.
Local restaurants supplied food
    faster than it could be eaten.
Even many of the victims were far more concerned
not with their own injuries
but with the fate of their friends and coworkers.

The selfless dedication and courage
of the rescue teams,
    medical personnel, and emergency crews,
the contributions of people from all over the country,
and the great love of family and friends
manifest the Spirit of God moving,
inspiring, and transforming
even such a horror as this
into a moment of grace.

Ron Howard's Academy Award-winning film *Apollo 13* is a
story of transfiguration—a desperate race against time becomes
NASA's "finest hour."

Even though history will never forget
    that week in April of 1970,
the film *Apollo 13* is a spellbinding story,
filled with nail-biting suspense.

On its way to the moon,
the Apollo spacecraft is crippled
when an oxygen tank on the command vehicle explodes.
Not only is the planned moon landing scrubbed,
but the mission suddenly becomes a race for survival.
Computer malfunctions, navigational problems,
the lack of heat and diminishing oxygen supply
    in the badly damaged spacecraft,
the threat of incineration upon reentry,
and the crew's deteriorating mental and physical condition
made the flight, as astronaut Jack Swigert says,
"like trying to drive a toaster through a car wash."

The NASA flight teams race against time,
and the technological magic it performs
to bring the three astronauts safely home
is a story of genuine heroism and courage.

The three astronauts,
mission specialists, engineers, and scientists
become a single entity of efficiency and ingenuity:
Commander Jim Lovell provides quiet but steady,
    intelligent, and compassionate leadership
    aboard the crippled spacecraft;
NASA technicians on the ground
calmly and methodically solve one crisis after another,
including ingeniously contriving a way to repair
the spacecraft's sophisticated ventilation system
using little more than cardboard and duct tape;
astronaut Ken Mattingly,
scrubbed from the mission because of a measles scare,
spends hours cramped inside
    a mock-up of the Apollo vehicle
devising a way to bring the spacecraft home
using a minimum amount of electrical power.
Even NASA's extended community
offers support to the astronauts' anxious families—
Neil Armstrong and Buzz Aldrin themselves
go to be with Lovell's elderly mother to reassure her
while she watched her son's plight unfold on television.

The faith and dedication of the mission team
are embodied in flight director Gene Kranz.
At one point in the film,
his NASA superiors are reviewing
all of the problems confronting *Apollo 13*
before they meet with the press.
"This is going to be NASA's biggest disaster ever,"
one official sighs.
Kranz overhears the comment and counters,
"With all due respect, sir,
I think this is going to be NASA's finest hour."

Through the same spirit of selfless generosity and unity,
we can transform the coldness,
sadness, and despair around us
on our part of the spaceship earth.

Stories of Saints and Prophets among Us

In every time and place, God's presence is revealed in the lives
and stories of everyday saints and prophets. These saints and
prophets among us demonstrate both the challenges and joys of
responding faithfully to the call to discipleship.

The story of Cardinal Joseph Bernardin's encounter with
Steven Cook, who falsely accused the cardinal of sexually
molesting him when Cook was a seminarian, is an inspiring
contemporary tale of the gospel call to forgiveness and reconciliation:

Imagine that someone you have never met
concocts an outrageous, monstrous lie about you.
Despite your claims of innocence,
you are publicly condemned, ridiculed, and demonized.
Only later, after your reputation is all but destroyed,
does the accuser recant.

Most of us would probably *not* respond
the way Cardinal Joseph Bernardin of Chicago did.

In 1993, a Philadelphia man named Steven Cook claimed,
in a CNN interview,
that he had been sexually abused by Cardinal Bernardin
when Cook was a seminary student
and Bernardin a priest.
Cook filed a ten-million-dollar lawsuit against the cardinal.
Cardinal Bernardin denied the allegations
and was vindicated a year later
when Steven Cook recanted the charges,

saying his recollections,
which were made under hypnosis,
were not reliable
and that he could no longer "in good conscience"
    pursue the charges.

But for Cardinal Bernardin, the matter was not closed.
Through intermediaries,
he contacted Steven Cook and asked to meet with him.
The meeting took place in Philadelphia
    on December 30, 1994.

Cardinal Bernardin wrote of the meeting:

"I began by telling Steven
that the only reason for requesting the meeting
was to bring closure
to the traumatic events of last winter
by personally letting him know
that I harbored no ill feelings toward him
and to pray for his physical and spiritual well-being.
He replied that he wanted to meet with me
to apologize for the embarrassment and hurt he had caused.
In other words,
we both sought reconciliation.

"Steven's apology was simple, direct, deeply moving.
I accepted his apology.
I told him that I prayed for him every day
and would continue to pray for his health and
    peace of mind.
It was very evident that he was in precarious health
[Cook had contracted AIDS]. . . .
It is a manifestation of God's love, forgiveness, and healing
that I will never forget."

After the meeting,
Cardinal Bernardin and Steven Cook
     celebrated the Eucharist
     for the Feast of the Holy Family.
"In my few remarks after the Gospel,"
Cardinal Bernardin remembered,
"I told him that in every family
there are times when there is hurt, anger, alienation.
But we cannot run away from our family.
We have only one family
and we must make every effort to be reconciled.

"Before Steven left,
he told me that a big burden had been lifted from him.
He felt healed and was at peace.
He also asked me to tell the story of his reconciliation
with the Church and with me.
I promised him I would
and that I would walk with him
in the weeks and months ahead.

"May this story of our meeting
be a source of joy and grace
to all who [hear] it."[2]

Cardinal Bernardin mirrors the father in the parable of the prodigal son (Luke 15:11–32). The father, who runs to greet and embrace his returning son even before the prodigal can begin his carefully rehearsed apology, is the model of the minister of reconciliation. The father welcomes his son joyfully and completely, with no recriminations, no conditions, no rancor. The opportunities we have to be ministers of reconciliation may not be as traumatic or dramatic as what the father in the parable and what Cardinal Bernardin faced, but our opportunities are no less potential moments of grace.

The saints and prophets among us come in all shapes, sizes, and ages, as the "bald eagles" of Oceanside, California prove. This story was widely reported in the media in the spring of 1994:

Last February, 11-year-old Ian O'Gorman
was diagnosed with non-Hodgkin's lymphoma
and began a series of chemotherapy treatments.
Ian decided to shave his head
    before all his hair fell out.
While in the hospital,
Ian's best friend, Taylor Herber, visited.
"At first I said I would shave my head as a joke,"
Taylor said.
"I thought it would be less traumatizing for Ian."

At school, Taylor told the other boys
what he was planning,
and they jumped on the bandwagon.
On March 11, 13 fifth-grade boys—
and their teacher at Lake Elementary School
in Oceanside, California—
marched into a hair salon
and got their own heads buzzed.
"Ian's a really nice kid,"
one of the them explained.
"We shaved our heads
because we didn't want him to feel left out."
Their teacher said,
"These kids did this all by themselves.
They're really good kids.
It was their own idea.
Their parents have been very supportive."

Ian said gratefully,
"What my friends did really made me feel stronger.
It helped me get through all of this.

I was really amazed
that they would do something like this for me."

The kids proudly call themselves the "Bald Eagles"
and vow that "when Ian gets his next CAT scan,
if they decide to do more chemotherapy,
we'll shave our heads for another nine weeks."[3]

The compassion and loving support that the "Bald Eagles" showed their pal Ian are nothing less than the Spirit of God, the love and presence of the risen Christ among us. Look around you: That same Spirit lives and breathes in the goodness of the saints and prophets in your world and community.

Stories of the Human Dimension of God's Word

Scripture, while the inspired Word of God, is still very much a human story. It is history, sociology, and anthropology, as well as theology. Sometimes the romance of the oft-told Gospel accounts masks the human realities of those events. But in those human dimensions of Scripture we discover God's love as well.

One Christmas Eve, a homilist offered this reflection on that night in Bethlehem so long ago:

No celebration of the year
appeals more to our senses than Christmas:
the *sight* of glittering lights,
the *taste* of the many delicacies of Yuletide feasting,
the *aroma* of freshly cut evergreen branches,
the *feel* of the crisp winter air and first snow,
the *sound* of the magnificent music of the season.

But that first Christmas had none of those things.
Consider the real sights and sounds and feels and tastes
—and *smells*—

experienced by the family of Joseph, Mary, and the child
on that night centuries ago:

the damp, aching cold
    of a cave along the Bethlehem hillside;
the burning in the eyes and throat
    from days of traveling on foot
    on hard, dusty roads;
the terror of finding yourself suddenly homeless,
    stranded, with no place to stay;
the paralyzing fear that robbers and wild animals
    could strike out of nowhere;
the silence of the night
    broken only by the cry of wolves
    and the bleating of sheep;
the anguish of a young woman
    delivering her first child alone,
    with her carpenter husband offering what help he can;
the overwhelming stench of a cave used as a barn:
    the smell of animals, manure, urine, and perspiration.

In life at its dreariest, ugliest, dirtiest, and messiest,
in life at its most terrorizing, hopeless, and painful,
God chose to enter human history and sanctify it.

Another homilist gave his listeners a look at the real Bethlehem of Jesus' time in a homily on the Fourth Sunday of
Advent:

Despite the romantic theme of the carol
"O Little Town of Bethlehem,"
Bethlehem would be one of the *last* places on earth
you would expect the long-awaited Messiah
    to make his appearance.

Ancient Bethlehem was a "bus stop"
      in the middle of nowhere.
Only a handful of people lived there permanently.
It was a rest stop
along antiquity's great caravan routes,
a place where people met quickly to conduct business,
grab a fast meal,
pick up fresh supplies,
change camels,
or spend a night during a long journey.

And yet,
the Gospels tell us,
it was in little, insignificant Bethlehem
that God chose to touch human history,
as human history moved hurriedly along.

The homilist then made the point that too often we let the busy little "Bethlehems" of our lives distract us from letting Christ—whose presence is often too quiet, too simple for us to realize—become part of our lives.

Filling in the blanks in a particular Gospel story can be an interesting exercise. Trying to imagine the untold story or details surrounding a particular Gospel story can help us better understand that Gospel's theme. In Luke 17:11–19, for example, Jesus cures ten lepers of their affliction and sends them off to show themselves to the priests. But only one returns to thank Jesus. That gave this homilist pause to wonder aloud:

So where *were* the other nine lepers who had been healed?

One of the now-clean lepers went off
to build a new life for himself.
He busied himself seeking work,
building a new place to live,
putting down roots for himself

and, maybe someday, a family.
Work, work, work
    became the driving force of his life.

But another one of the lepers was immediately overcome
with fear and worry—
"What do I do now?
I can't very well beg anymore.
I must find work.
But I have no skills,
I've never learned how to do anything.
Who will hire me?
How will I eat?"
So worried and fearful was the once-unclean leper
    for his future
that he was paralyzed from doing anything
and remained huddled at his old place at the city gate.

Still another leper,
realizing that he was now clean,
sought only one thing:
vengeance—
getting even with the many passersby
who laughed at him,
who ignored his pleas for help,
who inflicted so many cruelties and indignities on him
    because of his illness.
But the vengeance he craved proved to be
far more debilitating than his illness.

One of the lepers,
finally freed from his sufferings,
ran as far away from the place as he could.
All he wanted to do was forget his old life—
and everyone and everything about it.
He tried to make himself deaf to the cries

of the suffering of others,
but he could never run away far enough not to hear them.

And, of course, there was one leper
who went out and celebrated—
and celebrated and celebrated.
His newfound joy lasted as long as the wine did.
Once the wine and the camaraderie
        that comes with it disappeared,
he had to face a new life,
completely lost and alone.

There was one leper who didn't believe he was made clean.
Why would anyone—least of all God—
want to do this for him?
There had to be a catch.
So he just waited for his leprosy to return.
In his own mind and spirit,
he was never really healed.
And he wasn't.

And so the nine lepers went their separate ways.
But without a sense of gratitude
for the miracle they had experienced,
the miracle didn't last very long.
For their fears, their angers,
their repressions, their skepticisms,
their misplaced hopes and values,
just made them lepers all over again.

The missing element of the other nine's healings, the homilist offered, was a sense of gratitude to the God who, for no other reason than love too deep for mere human thought to fathom, breathes his life into us. The only fitting response we can make is to stand humbly before God in quiet, humble thanks—and yet, such an attitude of gratitude can transform cynicism and despair into optimism and hope and turn whatever good we do into experiences of grace.

"Epiphanies" and Moments of Grace within Larger Stories

In the precious few minutes a homilist has on Sunday, it is very difficult to reconstruct adequately the plots and subplots of the latest hit movie, play, or novel. Some exceptionally talented preachers occasionally do pull it off, but rarely. The challenge, of course, is to effectively retell the story so that anyone who has not seen the movie or read the book can grasp and appreciate the essence of the story without giving away the ending.

Often, however, there are moments within these larger stories—stories within stories, if you will—that can effectively express a dimension of faith. Here is one such moment in one of playwright Neil Simon's most enduring comedies:

Broadway Bound is the third play
in Neil Simon's trilogy about his coming of age
in a Jewish household in New York.

At one point in the play,
while talking to his mother,
Eugene (Simon's alter-ego) casually sits
on a corner of the family's dining room table.
His mother, Kate, immediately upbraids him:

"Are you crazy sitting on my dining room
table like that!?
I never want to see you show disrespect for this table!
My grandfather made this table
with his very own hands
for my grandmother.

Over 52 years she had this table.
When I was a little girl,
I'd go to her house,
and she would let me polish it.
I didn't know it was work—
I thought it was fun,
maybe because we did it together. . . .

"This table you eat on means everything.
It's the one time in the day
when the whole family is together.
This is where you share things—
people who eat out all the time don't get to be a family.
When I'm gone and you and your Josie get married,
this will be your table."[4]

Preaching on the Solemnity of the Body and Blood of Christ, this homilist built on mother Kate's insight to help the community see the altar in their church as the parish's "family table" at which we experience the peace and love of belonging to the family of God and to which we bring and share one another's joys, hope, and sorrows.

Sometimes a single character in a story can open up a dimension of spirituality:

One of the most delightful characters of the musical stage
is Tevye in *Fiddler on the Roof*.
Life for the poor Jewish milkman is a constant series
of travails, indignities and confrontations—
from the marriage of his three daughters
(the eldest to a poor tailor,
the second to a radical young student,
the third to a Gentile)
to the expulsion of his family from their Russian village.
But through it all,
Tevye maintains his faith in God.

Perhaps the most touching thing
about the character of Tevye
is his sense of prayer.
He leads his family in prayer each Sabbath
("May the Lord protect and defend you . . .").
The entire village comes together in prayer
for the wedding of his eldest daughter
("Sunrise, Sunset").

But throughout the play,
Tevye is constantly at prayer—
to Tevye, God is always present,
God is always there in his life.
As he delivers his milk and cheese,
Tevye talks out his problems with God
and asks God to help him understand
the purpose of the sufferings that befall him.
"Sometimes I think when things are too quiet up there,"
he tells God,
"You say to Yourself:
'Let's see, what kind of mischief
can I play on my friend Tevye?'"
Even Tevye's showstopper song, "If I Were a Rich Man,"
is a prayer to the Lord of all good things.

For Tevye, prayer is not just the formalized formulas
of his faith's "Tradition";
prayer is a constant awareness of God's presence,
an openness to seeing God
in the people and events around you.
Tevye prays with the understanding of Teresa of Avila,
who taught her sisters:
"Imagine the Lord himself at your side . . .
stay with this good friend as long as you can."

In every good story, a principal character will experience some kind of an "epiphany"—a single experience or series of experiences that will be a turning point in that character's life. That experience has a profound effect on the character, transforming his or her perspective or attitude, or leading to a new understanding that will have a lasting effect on him or her.

Like many moviegoers, the homilist of the following was moved by the "epiphany" experienced by Private James Francis Ryan in the final moments of the film *Saving Private Ryan*:

On the eve of D-Day 1944, three brothers—
the Ryans, an Iowa farm family—
are killed on different battlefields
    within days of one another.
When the allied command discovers
that there's a fourth Ryan brother out there somewhere,
the decision is made to find him
and return him home immediately to his grieving mother.
A squad of eight soldiers,
commanded by Captain John Miller,
is ordered to find and return Private James Ryan.

So begins what many are calling
the finest war movie ever made,
Steven Spielberg's *Saving Private Ryan*.
Captain Miller and his men
must forge behind enemy lines to find the surviving Ryan.
It is a dangerous, costly journey.
The platoon questions the sanity of its mission—
eight guys risking their lives to find one guy?
"Hey, we got mothers, too!" one soldier protests.
After they bury one of their buddies
who is killed by German sniper fire,
Captain Miller himself says,
"This Ryan better be worth it.

He better go home and cure some disease
or invent a new longer-lasting lightbulb or something."

Without giving away too much of the movie,
Private Ryan is found by Miller and his men.
But before they can head out,
Miller, Ryan, and the platoon must defend a strategic bridge
    against a German tank squad.
At the end of the battle,
Ryan is all too aware of the price
Miller and his men have paid
in order to find him and return him home.
Ryan asks the same question
the platoon has wondered from the beginning—
Is one guy worth all this?
The captain's parting words to Private Ryan
are this simple challenge:
"Earn this. Earn this."

We live our lives with the same realization and challenge now confronting young Private Ryan, the homilist continued. God breathes the gift of life into our beings and then sends us on our way to live lives worthy of the gift God has given us. The price of the life and love of God is the cross of compassion and justice. In working for reconciliation rather than conquest, in forgiving without limit or condition, in giving to others regardless of the cost or sacrifice to ourselves, we seek to "earn" the promise of Easter won for us by the Crucified One.

Stories about Finding the Extraordinary in the Ordinary

Great truths are often revealed in the simple things and unnoticed experiences of our everyday existence. Common, unremarkable objects and tasks can be metaphors of universal truths and profound realities. The books of Robert Fulghrum

(*All I Needed to Know I Learned in Kindergarten*) and Kathleen Norris (*Dakota, The Cloister Walk, Amazing Grace: A Vocabulary of Faith*), and the cartoons of Charles Schultz's *Peanuts* and Lynn Johnston's *For Better or For Worse* often illuminate life's most important truths in life's little noticed moments.

A chess game, for example, inspired one homilist to share this with his community on the last Sunday of the liturgical year, the Solemnity of Christ the King:

> In the game of chess,
> the object is to capture your opponent's king.
> You manipulate your own pieces,
> sacrificing your pawns and knights
> to protect your king,
> all the while strategically luring your opponent
> into making that one fatal move
> that will allow you to capture his king.
>
> In chess terms,
> Christ would make a lousy king-piece.
> While the chess master would march up the board
> taking fallen pieces,
> Christ the King would object:
> "No, don't take them,
> don't rejoice over their misfortune;
> lift them up,
> restore them to life and hope."
>
> Christ the King-piece would denounce
> the elaborate scheming to destroy the opponent—
> Christ the King-piece would demand
> that such energy be directed, instead,
> to building community
> and enabling peace, reconciliation, and justice
> to reign on the "board" that all sides share.
> Christ the King-piece would condemn

taking advantage of the other player's tragedy;
Christ the King-piece would challenge all the pieces—
black and white—
to support one another,
to care for one another,
to forgive one another,
without limits or conditions.
In fact, Christ the King-piece would refuse to label
pieces as "black" and "white,"
refuse to classify pieces
as pawns and knights and bishops and rooks;
refuse to recognize "sides."

Christ the King-piece would see only
one family on the chessboard,
brothers and sisters of the same Father.

In the following, the struggles faced by do-it-yourselfers illuminates the meaning of the Pentecost event:

For the "mechanically challenged" among us,
three of the most terrifying words
in the English language are
"Some assembly required."

We all have memories of Christmas Eves
struggling to put together our child's new bicycle,
of tables or desks that didn't quite come together
like the one pictured on the box,
of the nearly uncontrollable urge
to take a sledge hammer
to any number of appliances, stereos, and sports equipment
that, we were led to believe,
a six-year-old could assemble with only a screwdriver.
We all know someone
    who has been permanently traumatized

by a horrible encounter with a model airplane kit
    early in life.
And it is a matter of faith
that there is a special place in hell
for whoever devises those computer manuals—
the ones that come in five or six volumes
    of a zillion pages each.

But there are times—
too few times, perhaps—
when it all comes together:
when part A actually fits into slot B
and doohickey C snaps into place
    with whatchamaycallit D;
when all four legs of the table we assembled
stand straight and level;
when both stereo channels can be heard
    from our new system;
when even the computer works the way the manual
    (we think) says it would.
There is no more wonderful sense of accomplishment.
Oh, it may have taken a few more attempts
than we thought it would;
we may have had to start over a couple of hundred times;
we probably experienced a level of anguish and frustration
    we never imagined we were capable of.

But, in the end,
we understand the directions.
It all makes sense.
All the pieces fit.
It all comes together.

The Pentecost experience,
for the small gathering of Jesus' disciples,

is the moment when it all comes together for them:
when the life, death, and resurrection of Jesus
finally makes sense to them,
when the pieces of Jesus' teaching start to fit.

We can learn a great deal from the simple faith and goodness of children. A mother and her three-year-old daughter
playing a game together becomes an object lesson in generosity of spirit:

Three-year-old Katy barrels down the hall
clutching her new Candy Land game under her little arm.
It's a birthday gift,
Katy's first board game ever,
and she wants to play.
Her busy mother cannot resist her birthday girl's pleading,
so the two adjourn to Katy's room
and sit on the floor around the game board.

Mother and daughter begin to play,
each taking turns choosing from the color-coded cards
which tell them how many spaces
they can advance their little gingerbread pieces
on their way to the game's goal, the Candy Castle.

Much to the mother's dismay, however,
the game goes very badly for Katy.
While Mom has taken a big lead via Gumdrop Pass,
poor Katy is stuck in Molasses Swamp.
Mom tries to let Katy get ahead by not advancing her piece,
but Katy catches on.
"Mommy! You forgot to move your gingerbread man!
You've got to move so you can get to the Candy Castle!"
All too soon, the game is over—
Mom's gingerbread man has made it to the Candy Castle.

But before Mom can say, "I'm sorry, honey,"
Katy jumps up and lunges across the game board
to hug her mother.
The little girl is not disappointed but ecstatic.
"Mommy! You did it!
You got to Candy Castle!
You did it!"[5]

Little Katy's instinctive response to her mother's good fortune is not envy or disappointment or anger but joy, sheer joy at
her mother's good fortune. Children like Katy and Susie, in the
following story, can teach us a great deal about the reign of God:

He is sitting at his desk in his second-grade classroom.
Suddenly he is aware of a puddle between his feet
and the front of his pants are wet.
He cannot imagine how this could happen.
He is so embarrassed he wants to die.
When the guys find out,
he'll never hear the end of it;
the girls in the class will never speak to him again.
Please, dear God, he prays,
"I'm in big trouble. I need help now!"

He looks up from his prayer,
and a classmate named Susie
is carrying a gold fish bowl filled with water.
Suddenly she loses her grip of the bowl
and dumps the bowl right into the boy's lap.
The boy pretends to be angry—
but is praying to himself,
Thank you, Jesus! Thank you, Jesus!

Now, instead of being the object of ridicule,
the boy is enveloped in sympathy.
The teacher rushes him downstairs

and gives him gym shorts to put on while his pants dry out.
His classmates are on their hands and knees
cleaning up the mess.
But now it is poor Susie
who becomes the object of scorn.
She tries to help, but they tell her to get away.
"You klutz! What a dumb thing to do!"
And so it goes for the rest of the day:
He is surrounded by sympathetic friends
while poor Susie is shunned.

After school, the two are waiting for the bus.
Susie is standing off by herself.
He goes up to her and whispers,
"You did that on purpose, didn't you?"
Susie whispers back, "I wet my pants once, too."

"A Time to Laugh"

Humor is, arguably, the most effective story device—but also one of the most perilous. When a joke works, it's gangbusters; but when it bombs, the tremors can be felt for miles and hours. Some cautions are in order.

First, make sure that the joke is, in fact, funny, and that you can tell it "funny." Some people simply cannot tell a joke. Effective joke-telling demands confidence and a sense of timing. It is imperative that you practice telling the joke and become very comfortable relating it to an audience before using it as part of a homily.

Second, if you are going to use a funny story, make sure that nobody will be offended by the joke—nobody! If you suspect that someone—anyone—will be offended by the story or will not "get it," don't use it. Humor should be gentle; it does not have to sting or offend to be effective.

Finally, and by all means, make sure that the story can be "connected" to the Gospel you are preaching. Some clergy are regular comedians every Sunday; they're convinced that they have to start off with a few jokes and one-liners that have nothing to do with the Sunday Gospel in order to "warm up" the congregation to the point of the homily. The homilist may have them rolling in the aisles, but very little faith is being shared.

The following three stories reveal something of the ways and wonders of God. The first story was used in a homily on the parable of the talents (Luke 9:28–36):

The big animals challenged the little animals
to a football game.
By the end of the first half,
the big animals were way ahead of the little animals:
56-0.

At the start of the second half,
the big animals handed off the ball to the tiger;
but when the tiger reached the line of scrimmage,
down he went.
As he hobbled back to the huddle,
the big animals asked him, "What hit you?"
The shocked tiger said, "The centipede!"
Next, the big animals gave the ball to the lion.
The lion roared his way through to the line of scrimmage,
but down he went.
The other big animals asked him, "What hit you?"
The shocked lion answered, "The centipede!"
So the big animals gave the ball to the rhino.
He, too, thundered as far as the line of scrimmage
when he tumbled to the ground.
"What happened?" the big animals asked.
The rhino moaned in utter disbelief,
"It was that centipede!"

The big animals called a time-out.
They asked the coach of the little animals,

"Where was the centipede during the first half?"
The little animal's coach explained,
"In the locker room, lacing up his sneakers."

The homilist went on to hold up the centipede as a model of those faithful disciples who do not let their size or special need for more time to "lace up" stop them from contributing to the common good.

The second story is a retelling from the classic newspaper comic strip *Calvin and Hobbes*, by Bill Watterston:

The precocious Calvin of the comic strip
    Calvin and Hobbes
has a very difficult time staying out of trouble.
He and his best friend,
his stuffed tiger, Hobbes,
manage to create chaos of stupefying magnitude
for his parents, his teachers, and his classmates.

It will soon be Christmas
and Calvin is, of course, on his best behavior—
and it isn't easy.
But so far he's managing to stay out of trouble.
A few days before Christmas,
Calvin is outside in the yard.
He gathers up some snow and carefully crafts a snowball.
He gently places it on the ground
and begins to form another perfect snowball.
He places it next to the first one
and begins to make another.
And so on and so on.
His friend Hobbes is watching Calvin
make this gigantic pile of snowballs
and wonders what the mischievous Calvin is up to.
As he places what must be
the zillionth snowball in the pile,

Calvin says,
"The day after Christmas is going to be epic."[6]

And the day after Christmas, this homilist went on to remind his community, is indeed the beginning of an epic time. For long after the angels disappear into the heavens, the shepherds return to their flocks, the magi journey home, and the great star sets, Jesus remains. The Child in whom we rediscover God's great love for humanity becomes the adult Redeemer who challenges us to imitate his selflessness and compassion in order to transform our world in what can only be described as "epic." The miracle of Christmas should transform our lives, making the peace, justice, and hope of this holy season an "epic" reality in every season of the new year.

The third story offered a homilist a starting point for a reflection on God's invitation to conversion and redemption:

At Milan's famous La Scala opera house,
a tenor is making his debut in I Pagliacci.
When he sings the famous "Vesti la giubba" aria,
the response is so tremendous
that they can't go on with the opera
and he has to sing an encore.
And again.
In fact, he sings it eight times.
Finally he steps to the footlights
until the audience is completely quiet.
"My friends," he says,
"we have made history here tonight.
I say 'we' because it is certainly you, the audience,
    as much as I.
So far as I know, nobody in the history of La Scala,
not Martinelli, not Schipa, not Gigli, not even Caruso,
ever sang the "Vesti la giubba" more than six times.
And you, my dear friends, have caused me to sing it eight!
This is the greatest moment of my singing career—

I shall never forget you.
But—there is still the rest of the opera to perform
and my throat is becoming a bit tired.
So I ask you, dear friends,
do not ask me to sing this aria again."

From the gallery a member of the audience shouts,
"You'll sing it 'til you get it RIGHT!"

The homilist went on to make the point that, in Christ, God gives us a new vision and insight into our humanity and our world from which we can rebuild and remake the world into the kingdom of God. In Christ, we can start over again and again and again to remake our lives in God's love and transform our world in his justice—as many times as it takes us to "get it right."

Malcolm Muggeridge observed that "everything happening, great and small, is a parable whereby God speaks to us and the art of life is to get the message." Therein lies the art of preaching: to reveal God's presence through the stories of our human family. Dedicated and faithful homilists—who understand that preaching is a ministry to their people—are plugged into the world of their hearers and are both faithful and imaginative enough to find God in those stories.

Chapter 3

Connection: "The Word Made Flesh..."

Words are the instruments
with which we build our world—
our bridges to each other.
I cannot see your thoughts directly.
You must convey them to me, clumsily or well.
That is why we feel so frustrated
when words fail us at important moments,
when we feel we cannot reach another person
    despite our desire,
when we say, "I don't know what to say."
Yet we have seen those who do know what to say,
who animate the wavering,
who comfort the bereaved,
who inspire the hopeless,
who convert people, make them better, teach them.
And we know to our sorrow the contrary power of words
to inflame crowds or individuals,
to wound people,
to break off forever close human relations . . .
"Sticks and stone can break my bones
but words can never hurt me!"
We know better than that.
Words are not swords of lath
because they move the man who uses steel swords.

Garry Wills[1]

A bishop of London once asked a famous actor, "How is it that we preachers usually make little impression with the lofty and true subjects that we proclaim, whereas you actors on stage move people so much with your fictions?"

The actor replied, "It is because we speak of fictitious things as though they were true, whereas the clergy talk about true things as though they were fictitious."[2]

At the appointed time, the Gospels recount, God "humbled himself" and became human—one of us. Born to a poor carpenter and his wife, and given the name Jesus, the God-man experienced all the joys, pains, delights, trials, gratifications, and disappointments that are part of every human experience. In taking on our humanity in all its messy earthiness, God, tenacious in his love, became one with the people he continued to call to be his own.

The word that has come to explain this wonder, *incarnation,* comes from the Latin word meaning "enfleshing," "to be made flesh." In the incarnation, God became "enfleshed." The Eternal One touched human history in the person of Jesus and enabled humanity of every time and place to touch him, to know him, to encounter him in the reality of the human experience. Why? The fourth-century bishop Athanasius put this profound mystery so succinctly: "God became like us so that we might become like him."

To proclaim the reality of the Incarnate God to our communities, homilies must be "incarnational" as well. The homilist must "enflesh" the Word of God. God and humanity must touch in the homily; divine grace must connect with human reality in the preacher's words. As the U.S. Bishops' Committee on Priestly Life and Ministry wrote in *Fulfilled in Your Hearing,* the homilist must:

> . . . help people make the connections between the reality of their lives and the reality of the Gospel . . . help them see how God in Jesus Christ has entered and identified himself with the human realities of pain and happiness.

Jesus, God's perfect communication, knows how to make that critical connection with his hearers. He speaks to the people gathered on the banks of the Gennesaret and in the Temple precincts in words and concepts they can understand. He speaks to them, not in the words of the Pharisees or in the language of the rabbis, but in a way that employs images and pictures the people know all too well. In his stories, Jesus shows his hearers the unfathomable love of God present in their lives.

Today's homilists must mirror Jesus the preacher. Your words on Sunday should help the parish community see how God is present to them in their Monday-through-Saturday world. The core of the ministry of preaching is to make the Gospel story real to the community's own stories lived every day.

Connecting with your worshiping community begins by understanding the communication dimensions of homiletics. The next few pages focus on preaching as communication—a process of message design and transmittal—that *connects* the story of God's presence with the reality of your listeners' lives.

Why Preach?

In communications theory, every message designed and sent to an audience seeks one thing: *to affect the intended audience's behavior.* Quite simply, we communicate because we want someone *to do something.* Advertisers want the viewer or reader *to buy* their products; political candidates ask their constituents *to vote* for them; dedicated teachers want their students *to understand* a theory or process; comedians want their audiences simply *to laugh.*

Professional communicators understand that the success of a message is not determined by how creative the message is; rather, a message is successful *only if it elicits the specific response the message sender seeks from the intended audience.* The importance and value of a message, therefore, is determined *not* by the communicator sending the message but by the *audience*, in their acceptance and response to the message, or in their rejection (including their misunderstanding) of the message. Your homily last Sunday may have been a masterpiece of erudition, an oration of great wit and insight, but if the community failed to grasp, from the spoken word, the reality of God's presence in their lives, your homily failed.

So what are you trying to accomplish this Sunday? What do you want the audience *to do* in response to your message? In the story you tell your community:

- Do you want them *to understand or realize something* that they may not have thought about before?

- Do you want them *to respond to an appeal* for donations, volunteers, participation in a parish program?

- Do you want them *to take a stand and act upon that conviction* in a specific manner?

On most Sundays, the purpose of the homily is simply to help the community realize the presence of God in their lives. Sometimes, of course, a more specific response is sought. Whatever the hoped-for response, effective connecting begins by articulating clearly in your own mind what you—the homilist/communicator—want your audience to do.

As you plan your homily, focus your purpose on a single, clear idea. Limit yourself to a message that:

- you care about, that excites you, and that your audience will care about and be excited about;

- you can convey responsibly and completely in the time you have.

At a preaching workshop, ten deacons were assigned a five-minute talk on the theme of Christian marriage. The next week, eight of the ten tried to cover every aspect of marriage from the scriptural exhortation against divorce to the evil of living together to the legal process for obtaining a Church annulment. In trying to say in a few minutes everything that could be said about marriage, the eight preachers communicated little to their listeners.

Of the two other deacons, one spoke on the need for renewing the joys of marriage, and shared the story of how he and his wife make it a point to take out their wedding album and look through the pictures together every year on their anniversary. The second spoke on the importance of communications in marriage, stressing the value of making time just to talk to each other. Much was shared and communicated in those two limited but focused presentations.

A caution: Make sure the response you seek from your audience is something within its purview; do not ask or expect your listeners to do something they are unable or powerless to do, even if they want to. For example, the typical parish cannot do much about ending the international arms race—but, with grace, the community can transform its own fears, biases, and hatreds into trust, understanding, and compassion that are the basis for creating and nurturing community. Putting an end to the evil, pernicious pornography industry is probably not within your parish's reach either—but it can respect the human body as holy and sacred, made in the image and likeness of God, its Creator.

Knowing the Community

In all forms of advertising, publishing, and media production— from turning the latest Tom Clancy novel into a feature film to airing a new Bud Lite commercial—not a word is written, not a scene is shot, not a second of broadcast time is purchased, until a complete analysis of the audience is compiled: Whom does the advertiser want to reach? How old is the audience, where do they live, how educated are they, how much money do they earn? What images and ideas will the audience react to positively? What do they read, what do they watch? Who will come and see this movie—and are there enough of them to make the enterprise profitable? What actors bring this audience into the theater? How does the target audience feel about this product? Why do they use it? Why DON'T they use it?

The effective communicator begins by understanding:

- *who* must receive and understand the message if the objective is to be met;

- *why* this message is or should be important to them;

- what they *already know* about the subject of the message;

- what they *don't know but should know* about the subject;

- their *level of interest and investment* in the subject;

- their *attitudes*—pro and con—about the subject.

Product and advocacy advertisers discovered long ago that the most effective messages are those that are *audience-centered.* Messages must focus on an issue of concern to the intended audience and provide at least the beginning of the next step toward resolution of that issue. Effective messages focus on the target audience's needs and wants, not on the product or the issue being advertised, nor on the interests of the message's sender. Once the audience's needs are presented and validated in the advertisement, the product is then portrayed as the servant of those needs.

The same dynamics are at work in church on Sunday morning. The sad fact is that all of us listen and respond to messages only when we recognize that responding to this message is in our own best interests. We approach every communication with one principal question in mind: *Why is this important for me?* There has to be some clear benefit to listeners for investing their time and attention to this message. (Remember: The homily is just one of many messages competing for the congregation's attention every day.)

Like any message, if a homily is to have any meaningful impact on the Sunday congregation, it must be:

- *credible:* The story that is shared, the insights that are offered, must be believable to the hearer.

- *comprehendible:* The homily must be spoken in words and images that this particular assembly can understand. In communications theory, the message must be transmitted in a "code" that the receiver can "decode."

- *salient:* The message of the homily must be delivered in a manner that demands its audience's attention and captures their imagination.

- *pertinent:* The homily must be rooted in the experience of the community; it must be related to decisions and issues of concern to the congregation.

Like all forms of ministry, preaching is a form of "foot-washing." As Jesus removes his clothes, takes a towel and basin, and bends down to wash the feet of his disciples at the Last Supper, preaching demands putting aside your own comforting system of beliefs and attitudes that help you make sense of the world and trying to see the world through the eyes of your hearers, trying to understand, with compassion and without judgment, their attitudes, beliefs, and perceptions. It means becoming servant to the community, respecting and honoring its struggles, pains, and questions that it contends with every day. It means speaking in the language and concepts of your listeners and becoming involved, with them, in the grit and messiness of daily living.

Ironically, the wizards who create today's most successful advertising campaigns have embraced this idea of "foot-washing" in communications with more understanding and effectiveness than many of today's homilists. For example, think about a commercial you have seen or heard recently that you thought worked effectively—you might have purchased the product or service being promoted or perhaps you clipped the ad or jotted down the telephone number for future reference. (The very fact that you have remembered the ad indicates some measure of effectiveness.) Chances are this advertisement contained all of the five elements of an effective, persuasive message:

1. *The message got your attention.* The advertisement was placed in a magazine or program where you would find it (and the advertiser knew from the outset what kind of publications you read and programs you watch or listen to). The message then used words, images, and music that you would find attractive and interesting. Most importantly, the message presented a story (as the concept of *story* was discussed in the previous chapter) that involved you in the message.

2. *The message illustrated a problem you experienced or a need you identified with.* The message portrayed a problem in your life or appealed to a need you seek to fulfill.

3. *The message illustrated how to solve that problem or meet that need.* The message then showed you, quite convincingly, how the product or service in question would make your life so much better or how the candidate or position in question would make your city, state, nation, and/or the world a much better place. The message might have taken the approach of illustrating the advantages of the sponsor's approach to the problem or need or the evils that will befall you if you do not take the sponsor's approach.

4. *The message visualized the results.* The message portrayed how your problem would be solved, your need met, and/or the advantages to you if you use the advertiser's product or service.

5. *The message invited you to make a specific response.* The advertiser invited you to act—and made a point of showing you how easy it is to act as such: a simple telephone call, a visit to a web site, a convenient location with plenty of free parking. Or the advertiser included some extra inducement to act, heralded by such words as "free," "sale," "quantities are limited."

Connecting with your worshiping community begins by knowing the people who have gathered around the altar with you: families struggling to make ends meet; parents trying to create a loving home for their children despite the demands of jobs, school, and sports schedules; teenagers coping with the traumatic transition to adulthood; children riding a continuous merry-go-round of school, sports, and activities, trying to make sense out of a world that is both exciting and terrifying.

Trying to understand and deal with a set of values or concerns that may be the antithesis of what you believe is not easy. But the question is not what you, the homilist, would like the congregation to believe regarding the subject at hand or what attitude you believe your listeners should embrace; the question is what do *they*, in fact, *believe*, here and now? What is important to *them*? This is the "foot-washing" dimension of preaching: struggling to understand and honor their listeners' experiences, needs, problems, and hopes for themselves and their families, and showing them where and how God is present to them in the midst of their busy lives.

This is not to suggest that the Gospel message should be compromised or watered down for a given audience; the point is that connecting with the community begins with understanding their experience and reflecting how the Gospel lives within that experience. You must first meet your community where they are; then you and your community move ahead, together, to embrace a new spirit, a new understanding, a new discovery of God's presence. Making that connection requires the words of an understanding friend rather than a dogmatic theologian; it is expressed not in remote, exacting theological concepts but in images from the common, untidy, confusing world of every day.

"This Is the Acceptable Time..."

Every act of communication—including the Sunday homily—is affected by the physical limits of time and space. Every day of our lives we are bombarded with messages coming at us from all directions via computer programs, telephone lines, radio signals, and television channels. The electronic media has conditioned us to absorb information in thirty-second bite-size pieces. The price of such marvelous technology has been the constriction of our ability to pay attention to so much information. Television is especially responsible for the shorter attention span of audiences of all ages.

Consider the following:

- The typical television commercial is thirty seconds in length; the standard commercial on radio is one minute. Many major-market stations also offer ten- and fifteen-second messages.

- The lead story on the television news each evening is usually little more than two minutes in length; the average story, with video clips, is less than one minute.

- On a television sitcom or drama series, most scenes are written for about two minutes in length, so that the scene changes frequently (a technique learned from music videos).

- Radio programming—newscasts, commercials, feature reports, commentaries—is written and presented in segments of fifteen, thirty, and sixty (maximum) seconds in length.

- Studies conducted by American University in Washington, D.C., indicate that the average television viewer digests only one third of the main points in a given television program.[3]

- According to *Business Week*, the typical business executive has an on-the-job attention span of six minutes. Every six minutes something happens to disrupt the executive's attention span: a telephone call, an unplanned meeting, a situation demanding an immediate decision.[4]

That doesn't mean that the art of rhetoric is lost forever; it does mean that if you want to communicate faith from the pulpit you have to realize at the start that in our high-tech media-oriented society your community's attention span is quite limited. People simply will not sit and listen for long periods of time. Few homilists are naturally fascinating, funny, and entertaining enough to keep a congregation enthralled for more than a few minutes.

So *time*—not how much time the rubrics specify but how much time the congregation gives you before that remote clicker we all have inside our brains zaps you off—is a major consideration in planning and delivering a homily that connects with your community.

Another communication consideration is *context*—the psychological dynamics between the communicator and the receiver of a message. Every act of communicating begins with a basic understanding on the part of the audience regarding its relationship with the communicator. When prospective customers walk into a car dealership, for example, they understand that the sales representative's warm welcome and friendliness are part of the ploy to get them to buy a new car. College students go to classes with the understanding that their professors know what they are talking about; they take notes, complete the assignments, and study for exams with the understanding that, if they do well, they will receive a good grade. Theater goers come to see the latest Neil Simon play expecting to be entertained. When the boundaries of a situation's context are crossed—the sales rep becomes rude or pushy, the professor is not prepared for class, the play is not funny or becomes pretentiously preachy—the message-sending process fails.

Worship and preaching also take place within a context. Members of the congregation enter the experience with certain expectations: that they will encounter the holy, that they will be enriched by the experience, that they will be welcomed despite their doubts, hurts, and misgivings. They have basic expectations of their preachers: that they will be prepared, kind, and respectful, that they will speak with honesty and integrity, and that they at least try to live what they preach.

Certain occasions dictate special contextual considerations, of course. Presiding and preaching at funeral liturgies, for example, demand sensitivity, compassion, and a sense of dignity; to begin the homily at a funeral Mass for someone's mother with a hilarious joke will, to say the least, betray the family's trust. Using a couple's wedding as a forum for indicting a culture that undermines the family and countenances the breakdown of so many marriages is to rob the couple and their families of the joy of this celebration that rightly belongs to them.

Sacred Space

The place in which we gather to worship is sacred space. But the shape, size, and arrangement of various components—the "feel" of that space—can affect your ability to connect with the community.

First, consider the size of your audience. If the liturgy is going to be celebrated by a small group of people, you want to avoid becoming too formal or too removed from the gathering. Conversely, you cannot very well sit down at the edge of the sanctuary and "chat" with a congregation of five or six hundred worshipers.

Another consideration is the specific place from which you will speak. Can you see and be seen by everyone in the congregation? Is there proper lighting in the sanctuary so the congregation can see you and you can see your notes? Is there a public address system that works without calling attention to itself, that amplifies without overpowering?

A critical but often overlooked question deals with the arrangement of the church. For example, does it enhance or undermine the creating of prayerful community? Does the seating arrangement create or destroy the sense of community? (Fifty or sixty people scattered throughout a church built for four hundred can be a nightmare for the celebrant/homilist.) Does the decor of the worship space—simple and quiet yet beautiful in design—invite prayer, or is the decor so busy with color and cluttered with furnishings that the space is an accumulation of disjointed, unfocused distractions? What about the "feel" of the church and the liturgy? Is an attitude of prayer encouraged by respectful silence, or is the church and the liturgy busy with a rush of frantic movement and a barrage of sound? Is the liturgy celebrated in a relaxed, reverent, thoughtful manner, or is the operating philosophy "keep it moving"?

Some sanctuaries are ideally designed for large festive liturgies with throngs of worshipers and a procession of ministers, but in that same space, a smaller, more intimate gathering is lost. Some smaller churches, on the other hand, are little more than concrete boxes designed to be used for so many purposes that they fail to fulfill any of them well.

An important consideration, too, is the physical comfort of the congregation. Those rickety metal folding chairs common to every church in the country have done more to destroy the preaching craft than the most incompetent preachers. Long, stiff, hard wooden benches do not help, either. Neither a congregation shivering to keep warm nor one wilting in the heat will be very receptive to a homilist's message. In all probability, there may not be much that you can do about the physical environment, but to be forewarned is to be forearmed.

Connecting with your worshiping community demands a conscious effort. To connect effectively the reality of God's love with the everyday reality of the community begins with understanding the ministerial dimensions of preaching: to love those in your community enough to listen to them, to travel with them on their journeys, to honor their struggles to live faithfully in a world that seems to be working overtime to sterilize itself of God's presence.

Homily #1: Sometimes a parent can surprise you

The preachers of the following three homilies were particularly effective in connecting with their communities. The first homily was preached on the call of the first disciples, recounted in Luke's Gospel (5:1–11). Jesus has just come upon Peter and his brothers washing their fishing nets. He asks them to row out a short distance and cast their nets into deep water. Despite their misgivings, Peter directs his men to let down the nets into the deep water—and, sure enough, they catch so many fish that the nets begin to break. Returning to shore, Peter drops to his knees before Jesus: "Go away from me, Lord, for I am a sinful man." Jesus replies: "Do not be afraid; from now on you will be catching people."

Jesus' words to Peter have inspired many sermons on the call to be evangelizers of the Gospel and the gift of a vocation to the priesthood or the religious life. But on this particular Sunday, the homilist was struck by Peter's initial refusal of Jesus' invitation and saw an important connection for the families in his community. He told this *story:*

The teenager had her driver's license
for only a few weeks.
After much pleading,
Dad relented and let her use the family's new car
to take her friends to the beach.

She was very careful.
She kept under the speed limit all the way.
She took great pains to park the car in a safe spot.

But on the trip home, *crunch!*
She never saw the other car.
In an instant,
the front bumper, headlight, and part of the door
were reduced to a crumbled mass of metal.
She wanted to die.
Dad would have her head.
Might as well burn my driver's license, she thought.
I'll be grounded until I'm old enough for social security.
And so she limped home in her father's
      once-beautiful automobile,
dreading the reception that awaited her.

As she pulled into the driveway,
her parents were waiting in the doorway.
When they saw her drive up, they both ran outside.
From the looks on their faces,
she knew this would not be a happy homecoming.
Dad ran ahead of Mom—
and right pass the damage.
He took his daughter's hand
and helped her out of the car.

"Dad, I'm sorry," she stammered.
But he wouldn't let her finish.

"Are you all right? Were you hurt? Was anybody hurt?"
he wanted to know, hugging her tighter and tighter.

She smiled—
and began to cry—
grateful that her dad was so understanding—
and a little ashamed
that she had expected so little from him.

Every parent and child know this story (and some undoubt-
edly wished their own version of the homilist's tale ended as
happily). Then the homilist made the *connection:*

That has happened to all of us—
just when we expected our parents
or spouse or friend or boss or client
to kill us for something we had done—or not done—
they reacted with understanding, compassion,
and immediate forgiveness.

So it is with God,
who always welcomes us back,
without condition or limit.
We sometimes expect too little
from our relationship with God.

Like Peter in today's Gospel,
many of us suffer from an "inferiority complex"
when it comes to God—
we're neither good enough
nor wise enough in church protocol
to consider ourselves "religious."
Having seen what some people
        have done to the word *Christian,*
we're too embarrassed to use the word
        to describe ourselves.

Like Peter, we shy away from God
because we cannot imagine
how God could possibly love sinful, godless us.
But that is the "mystery" of God—
that God loves us despite ourselves.

Thomas Merton observed that
"the root of Christian love is not the will to love
but the faith that one is loved by God
. . . irrespective of one's worth.
In the true Christian vision of God's love,
the idea of worthiness loses significance.
The revelation of the mercy of God
makes the problem of worthiness
    something almost laughable . . .
no one could ever, alone,
be strictly worthy to be loved with such a love—
[such a realization] is a true liberation of spirit."

This homilist understood the reality of doubt in the faith of
his hearers. He knew all too well that God can seem buried in
the midst of religious practices whose meanings can become
lost in rote repetition. He had probably experienced that sense
of worthlessness in his own life when confronted with the
example of Jesus and the heroic witness of those saints who
have followed him throughout history. At some time in his life,
the preacher, too, had been hesitant to utter the name of God
publicly for fear of ridicule, or had backed away from the opportunity to do something that was labeled "religious."

In his closing *invitation*, the homilist repeated Jesus' words:

As Jesus reassures the terrified Peter,
Jesus reassures us:
Do not be afraid.

Do not be afraid
that you are not good enough—
for God has created each one of us
    with a piece of his goodness within us.

Do not be afraid
that you do not have enough to give—
all God asks is that you do what you can
    with what you have.

Do not be afraid
that you are not successful enough—
for God measures the heart, not the results.

Do not be afraid
that you are not loud enough in your praise
or demonstrative in your religion—
for God is praised most fully
in the quiet, loving kindness we extend to one another.

Do not be afraid
that you lack the courage or generosity to be a saint—
for God gives us the grace to make miracles happen
in the most ordinary of circumstances.

Do not be afraid
that you are not loving enough—
for God loves enough for all of us.

Homily #2: Aunt Elizabeth's special recipe

The following was preached at a first Eucharist liturgy for second graders. Although not theologically sophisticated, it is nonetheless a sound, meaningful explanation of the Eucharist that can be grasped by seven- and eight-year-olds.

The homilist began with a *story* about his beloved Aunt Elizabeth:

> When my brothers and sisters and I were kids,
> we always loved going to Aunt Elizabeth's house.
> She was a wonderful woman—my grandmother's sister.
> Aunt Elizabeth's small house was always filled
> with love, joy, good times—
> and wonderful cinnamon-swirl cookies.
>
> She made them from scratch—
> shortbread cookies with swirls of delicious cinnamon.
> Whenever we went to visit,
> there was always a jar full of her special cookies.
>
> I remember when Aunt Elizabeth was in her eighties:
> The simplest tasks took more time
> and demanded more energy
> than when she was a younger woman.
> But, on days when she knew we would be coming to visit,
> she would get up very early
> and plant herself in her beloved kitchen.
> Her hands, gnarled by arthritis,
> would carefully mix the batter,
> blend in the sweet cinnamon swirl,
> cut the dough in almost perfect circles,
> and put them in the oven.
>
> The work demanded so much of her, physically—
> but, as she told us every time she served those cookies,
> the joy they brought to us made it all worthwhile.
> We all realized the effort it took her—
> and that made the cinnamon delights all the more special.
> But we would never dare suggest
>   that she stop making them—
> because Aunt Elizabeth's cinnamon cookies

contained much more than
the flour, sugar, eggs, water, cinnamon,
     and other ingredients.

In her loving preparation of those cookies
for the people she loved most,
Aunt Elizabeth included a most special ingredient—
a piece of herself,
her love.

The homilist then quite naturally moved on to *connect*
Aunt Elizabeth's love for her family in struggling to bake their
favorite cookies with the redeeming love of Christ contained
in the sacrament of the Eucharist:

I think of Aunt Elizabeth
every time I go to communion.
Because, in much the same way
that Aunt Elizabeth put a piece of herself
in the cookies she lovingly baked for us,
Jesus has put a piece of himself
in the bread and wine of the Eucharist.

Maybe you've experienced the same thing:
Did you ever work so hard on something for someone—
like making a gift or a card for your mom or dad—
that you really felt that
there was a piece of yourself in the gift,
that your love was as much a part of the gift
as the paint and the wood
     and the time you put into making the gift?

It's the same with the Communion:
Jesus loves us so much that
he lived for us, died for us, and rose for us.
And now he places "a piece of himself"

in this bread and wine,
and invites us to celebrate with this food
until we take our places at the great banquet of heaven.

In receiving Jesus in the Eucharist
we become what we receive:
We become the one body of Christ,
we become family to one another.

The concluding *invitation* was exactly that—an invitation
to the feast:

So come to Jesus' table as often as you can.
As we heard in the gospel story,
we are always welcomed here by Jesus.
When you feel happy,
when you feel sad,
when you are celebrating the great moments of life,
when you are mourning or in pain—
come to Jesus' feast.

His love is right here in this bread and wine.

And when we receive him in the Eucharist,
Jesus' love [*the homilist points to his heart*]
is right here.

Homily #3: *Leaven in the midst of destruction*

A preacher who was attuned to the world around him and
in touch with the reality of his community made Jesus' short
parable on yeast (Matthew 13:33) a part of that world and reality. The *story*:

In the midst of tragedy and devastation,
moments of real grace can be found.

Two stories you may have heard this week
about young people bringing such new life
to the horror they found around them:

In May, severe tornadoes and twisters
destroyed whole neighborhoods in Oklahoma.
Many of the students at Del City High School
    and their families
lost everything they owned
when tornadoes reduced their neighborhoods
    into splinters.
When the students at their cross-town rival,
Edmond North High School,
learned that the Del City students
had nothing to wear for their prom,
Edmond North went to work.
Following their own prom,
the Edmond North students collected
    more than 600 gowns,
along with shoes, makeup, and purses,
and recruited a local tuxedo shop
to provide formal wear for the boys.
The Edmond students then turned their school
    into a boutique
where Del City students could pick out
    their gowns, shoes, and makeup.
Because of the Edmond students' kindness and hard work,
Del City's prom lived up to its theme,
"A Night to Remember."

Last month, an American Airlines MD-80,
trying to land in Little Rock during a severe thunderstorm,
slid off the runway
and tore open when it hit a lighting tower.
Nine people, including the captain, were killed—
but 136 others survived,

many because of a group of college students
    who were on the flight.
The Ouachita Baptist University Choir
was returning to Arkansas
    after a two-week tour of Europe,
where they sang for and prayed with Kosovo refugees.
The students pulled survivors through
    a hole in the plane's fuselage,
carried the severely injured out of the wreckage
    on their backs,
and led terrified and confused passengers
    out of the plane and through the storm to safety.
As one of the Ouachita students said,
"We knew what we had to do to help each other.
Everyone on that plane came together as a family"—
a family led by a group of college students
who soothed souls on one continent
and saved lives back home.

The homilist then *connects* the story to his listeners' world
with the key question:

What in the world
would lead a group of students to give up
their expensive prom dresses
and work countless hours
to save the prom of students they don't even know?

What in the world would compel students
to risk being incinerated
in order to make sure others reach safety first?

It is that sense of compassion within our hearts
that makes us fully human,
that sense of compassion
that connects us to one another as brothers and sisters,

that sense of compassion
that is fully immersed in the love of God.

That compassion and connection is the "yeast"
that Jesus speaks of in today's Gospel—
the "yeast" that makes our lives and communities
rise above the tragedies and devastation
(often of our own making),
transforming such sadness into joy,
such despair into hope,
such death into life.

The *invitation:*

Jesus calls us to be such "yeast"
in our own village of the kingdom.
Jesus does not ask us to be hammers of judgment
nor seers of condemnation;
he asks us to be simple "leaven,"
that in our own small ways
we may make God's love rise among us.

In becoming "yeast" for others,
Jesus assures us,
the more complicated things will be transformed.
In our home and workplaces,
in our schools and playgrounds,
in every place, in every time,
may we seek to become "yeast"
for a world desperate
for the "leavening" grace and healing
    of the kingdom of God.

In her book *Amazing Grace: A Vocabulary of Faith*, Kathleen Norris offers this insight to preachers who seek to connect with their hearers in the stories they tell:

> Sermons point to a relationship with a God who has promised to be present when two or three are gathered in his name. This is Jesus, whom Christians refer to as the Word incarnate, the Word made flesh. And, as people come to church to renew and sanctify their lives, only a living word will do.[5]

CHAPTER 4

INVITATION: "YOUR ATTITUDE MUST BE CHRIST'S"

Jesus constantly does the most unexpected things,
revolutionizing the accepted norms of conduct.

He praises pagans and prostitutes,
draws near to Samaritans and lepers.
He attacks the most respected classes
and insults his hosts at dinner.

In the midst of intense labors
he finds time to welcome little children. . . .
He rebukes the wind and the waves
and falls silent before his accusers.
Men would never have fabricated such a . . . religious leader,
and precisely for this reason
the gospels have undying power to convert humble hearts.
This spendthrift charity is properly divine.
This is what God must really be,
and if he were to become man,
this is how he would behave.

Avery Dulles
Apologetics and the Biblical Christ[1]

Jesus does not hang around with the "cream" of Jerusalem society; rather, the crowds who gather to listen to Jesus consist of
fishermen, laborers, shepherds, tax collectors, peasants, and

prostitutes. When concern is raised about the class of people he is attracting, Jesus responds that it is exactly to these poor sinners that he has come to bring salvation.

But in reading the Gospels, one suspects that Jesus actually likes and cares about these people. Jesus sees something special in each of them—Matthew, the despised tax collector; the notorious Samaritan woman at Jacob's well; the hotheaded sons of Zebedee; Peter, the gruff fisherman; the strange little man, Zacchaeus, who climbs the sycamore tree to see Jesus; scruffy little children. Jesus seeks to bring out the good that exists within each of them. He calls them to redemption and discipleship, and challenges them to conversion in preparation for his Father's reign.

But first, Jesus *loves* them.

He *cares* about them.

He *accepts* them for what they are—very imperfect people, people who have made messes out of their lives, people who struggle to make sense out of their existence, people too overwhelmed by the demands of this life to worry about the next. Despite their obtuseness, their failures, their sins, Jesus welcomes them all.

And that is the great paradox of the Gospel: that despite all the selfish and mean-spirited things we do, God never stops loving and caring about us. God never ceases to call us back, never gives up seeking us out.

The homilist's message should be centered in that same love of God, in that same attitude of welcome to all who gather in his Son's name. The *invitation* to embrace and be embraced by that love is the third dimension of the *story/connection/ invitation* homiletics model.

The Words of Invitation

Strategically, the same thought and care that goes into the *story* (the introduction) of the homily should go into the *invitation* (the conclusion). As the final words of the homily, the effective invitation:

- should make clear to the listeners what is being asked of them: realistic and practical responses they can make to the Word just proclaimed or how they can and should respond to the appeal the homilist has made to them;

- refers back to the introduction, tying the whole homily together: referring back to that opening story to make the point of the homily unmistakably clear to the community;

- ends with what professional speechwriters call a *clincher* —a memorable, thought-provoking exit line.

Too many presentations, including homilies, have little impact because they fail to ask the audience to do anything. In his acclaimed book on the art of presentations, titled *"I Can See You Naked,"* speech coach Ron Hoff recalls asking an ex-boss what he wanted to accomplish in an upcoming speech. He said, "Oh, I just wanted to open up their minds."

Hoff's response: "Fine. Great. Admirable. But most people are not sitting around waiting to have their minds opened up. They are waiting for you to drive home a specific point or idea that they can really use."[2]

The same holds true for the Sunday homily. Exactly what are you inviting the people in your faith community to do that will make their lives better? Have you made the specifics of that invitation clear to them? And are you leaving them in the right frame of mind, the right disposition of heart and spirit, to respond to your invitation?

Embracing the Attitude in Invitation

Invitation is, first, an attitude. The sincerity of the speaker, his/her conviction that God speaks his Word of love in Scripture and sacrament, raises the homily above the level of pep talk. Such sincerity, passion, conviction, and caring are not revealed in words alone but in the tone of the voice, the expressions of the body, the joy in the eyes. Make no mistake: Your listeners can "read" your attitude quickly and accurately, regardless of the words coming out of your mouth.

And sometimes your audience will read attitudes you do *not* intend to project but they, nonetheless, read accurately. Every audience can perceive pomposity, arrogance, bigotry, self-righteousness, and anger in a guilty speaker or presenter. As a homilist, your attitude is a reflection of your heart and spirit.

So before taking on the ministry of preaching, wise homilists spend some time reading their own heart and spirit regarding their attitudes—attitudes toward:

- preaching itself: *Is this a ministry or an obligation? What am I more concerned about: sharing faith or keeping it short?*

- the community: *Do I love these people as fellow pilgrims? Do I care about them? Do I respect the struggle, the pain, the confusion in their lives—even though I may not understand it or may have difficulty relating to it in my own life? Do I see these people as a community of individuals or the "mass" at Mass? Do I consider it a privilege to be their pastor or are these sheep lucky to have me as their pastor?*

- the Word of God: *Do I hear God speaking to me in this passage from Scripture? Do I understand its demands on me as well as on my hearers?*

Again, Jesus serves as the model preacher for all homilists: Jesus speaks in words and symbols that his Palestine audience of neither education nor sophistication can grasp and embrace. Even in admonishing his listeners, Jesus' love and compassion cannot be missed. Jesus' parables and teachings are grounded in the simple yet profound reality that God is our Father who loves us and never stops loving us.

Every homilist should take to heart what the apostle Paul wrote to the young church at Philippi: "Your attitude must be like that of Christ" (Philippians 2:5)—humble before God's love, empty of all conceit before one's brothers and sisters, optimistic in the victory of the cross and the miracle of Easter's empty tomb.

The "Verbals" of Preaching: The Text

A homily is made up of both the *verbal* (the words and the text) and the *nonverbal* (vocal emphasis and tone, physical gestures, and attitude). Both the verbal and nonverbal must work together to convey that attitude of invitation.

For every speaker, words are the tools of the craft. If the homily is to connect the Gospel of Jesus to the everyday experience of your listeners, the words of your homily must be incarnational—your words must "enflesh" the Word made flesh.

As you think through your homily, you will be scribbling notes and jotting down ideas. Some writers keep journals and notebooks, some jot ideas down on separate note cards, and some very good writers can capture such flashes of creativity on whatever paper is handy at the moment—wastebasket scraps, napkins, the corners of the telephone book, used envelopes.

At some point, you will sit down and write your homily. Especially if you are a novice homilist, write out the entire homily using the exact words you would like to use. Later, as you practice delivering your homily, you can reduce the text to notes.

The main objective in writing your text is to keep your sentences "sayable." When you begin putting words to paper, you may very well start writing in the style and form many people employ when they communicate in written form: long, complex sentences with a myriad of words and a maze of clauses. When we take pen to paper, we are usually writing for the eye.

But writing a speech is to write for the ear—and not the writer's ear but the audience's. Remember that your listeners will be trying to absorb what you say and, if your sentences are too dense with information and abstract concepts, they will not be able to follow your ideas. Listeners will not have a printed copy that they can refer to in order to check anything they may have missed or clear up any misunderstandings or doubts they may have. All they have is you up there at the lectern—and so your words must be "hearable" and comprehensible the first time out.

Begin by structuring your sentences in the active voice— subject/verb/direct object—and avoid adding clauses and complex qualifications. Rather than cluttering your sentences with long explanations and layers of adjectives and adverbs, use words that have precise meanings: cobalt instead of "blue"; "hurried" instead of "went quickly "; "shouted" instead of "said loudly"; "pleaded" instead of "asked." (When you use the speechwriter's indispensable tool, *Roget's Thesaurus*, you are not looking for the most impressive word but the most precise word.)

The words you choose must also be "sayable" for your sake as well. The words have to be you. You—NOT the text—are the medium of communications here; so you have to be able to articulate this text clearly. Words that you have difficulty pronouncing, sentences that trip you up, images that become obscure or murky in their explanations, will not connect with your hearers.

So as you write, do not write as a writer; rather, write as a *speaker*. Read your text out loud as you write to keep your sentences crisp and sharp.

In the writing process, pay particular attention to the opening story and concluding invitation. The story should be constructed clearly, completely, and concisely so that the audience will follow each element as the story unfolds; the words should paint a picture in the listeners' minds. As much care should go into the invitation that concludes the homily, especially the last line. The final words of your homily should express your conviction and hope in the promise of the empty tomb despite the reality of the cross; the words should invite your hearers to embrace the love of God that your story has shown them in their midst. Give particular time and attention to your last line, the "clincher": make your last words to the community memorable, thoughtful, and insightful.

Two presentation techniques used by professional speech-writers can be used effectively in homilies, as well:

Repetition: repeating a key word or phrase for emphasis. Jesus uses this technique in the Sermon on the Mount in Matthew 5:3–11, in introducing each of the beatitudes with the words "Blessed are . . ." In his famous speech at the 1963 March on Washington, Dr. Martin Luther King's repetition of the phrase "I have a dream" effectively invited a nation to embrace that dream:

I have a dream
that one day this nation will rise up and live out
the true meaning of its creed:
"We hold these truths to be self-evident
that all men are created equal."

I have a dream
that one day out of the red hills of Georgia
the sons of former slaves
and the sons of former slaveholders
will be able to sit down together
at the table of brotherhood.

I have a dream
that one day even the state of Mississippi,
a state sweltering in the heat of oppression,
will be transformed into an oasis of freedom and justice.

I have a dream
that my four children will one day live in a nation
where they will not be judged by the color of their skin
but by the content of their character.

Parallel construction: using a consistent word pattern to connect several related points or ideas, making them more conspicuous and memorable to listeners. Look at the way Jesus structures the parable of the sheep and the goats (Matthew 25:31–46); both the invitation to the sheep and the cursing of the goats, as well as their responses to the king's judgment, use the same words and sentence structure, making the words especially memorable to the audience.

Abraham Lincoln used this technique quite effectively in the conclusion to his second inaugural address:

> With malice toward none,
> with charity for all,
> with firmness in the right
>   as God gives us to see the right,
> let us strive on
> to finish the work we are in,
> to bind up the nation's wounds,
> to care for him who shall have borne the battle
>   and for his widow and orphan,
> to do all which may achieve and cherish
>   a just and lasting peace
>   among ourselves and with all nations.

As you draft your homily, read you words out loud. You will "hear" for yourself how your words flow; you will "hear" places where repetition and construction will make your words more memorable; you will "hear" the places where you should speak faster, slower, pause; you will "hear" the trouble spots that need "defogging."

Peggy Noonan, the former CBS news producer who has written speeches for two U.S. presidents and several Fortune 500 CEOs, writes that "we have gained a sense in our lives that true things are usually said straight and plain and direct."[3] "Enflesh" the Word of God, then, in words that are simple, direct, and declarative.

The "Nonverbals" of Preaching:
The Human Voice and Body

Dr. Thomas Long of Princeton Theological Seminary notes that television has reduced some preaching to "sound-bytes, imagistic bursts, and episodic narratives" but that, despite the technology at our disposal "the most powerful form of communication is still one human being standing up and speaking courageous truth."[4]

The very act of "standing up" is as critical in the communication exercise as the words of truth enunciated. If preaching were a matter of finding the words alone, then why not just photocopy the text of the homily and pass them out after the Gospel? Because the physical presence of the homilist gives life and power and force to those words. Ineffective speakers underestimate their role as the vehicle or channel of communications in public speaking. They do not understand that the nonverbal elements of a speech—the speaker's voice and body—communicate as much as their words.

Preaching, especially the concept of invitation, is more than saying the right words. To preach in a way that is faithful to the ministry of invitation means knowing how to express those words, realizing the effect of your nonverbals on your listeners.

The Human Voice

Ralph Waldo Emerson wrote that "nothing great is achieved without enthusiasm." Enthusiasm, passion, and conviction are all reflected in the tone of a speaker's voice.

Think about the last time you listened to someone whose voice had a certain "edge" to it. Or perhaps someone responded to your greeting with a simple "Hello" in which you unmistakably "heard" worry or sadness or nervousness, and you instinctively asked "What's wrong?" Or perhaps you were served by a waiter or clerk who said all the right words but whose coldness and lack of grace left you feeling insulted and angry, making you feel like a pest rather than a guest.

That same "edge" can be detected in every homilist's and presenter's vocal tone. If you are upset, tired, angry, or nervous, it will be evident in the tone of your voice. That same tone is heard in the celebrant's or presider's voice not only in the homily, but in the greeting, in the proclamation of the Gospel, in the invitation to pray, and in the offering of the Eucharistic Prayer. Some speakers who are skilled actors do manage to hide negative feelings or emotions, but for most of us, the tone of our voices—as well as our eyes, faces, and bodies (shaking, twitching, etc.) will betray those feelings. Positive emotions— joy, excitement, sincerity—are also revealed in the tone of the speaker's voice. Regardless of the words in the text they are hearing, listeners will detect your true feelings and attitudes in the tone of your voice. It will be immediately apparent in your tone that you are merely fulfilling a chore demanded by the rubrics of the liturgy—or that you truly care about what you are preaching and the community you are addressing.

Emerson's dictum on enthusiasm, then, is critical to every homilist.

The human voice also possesses a number of other properties that enhance a speaker's message:

Articulation, pronunciation, and enunciation: Articulation is the physical ability to make the sounds that the audience will recognize as words. *Pronunciation* is the correct way to pronounce a word. (The word *nuclear* said as *nucular* and *perspiration* said as *prespiration* are examples of mispronounced words). *Enunciation* is the clarity in which a speaker actually says those correctly pronounced words (examples of poor enunciation: *guvment* for *government, gonna* for *going to,* and *singin'* for *singing*).

A problem for many speakers is dropping the sounds of the last consonants of words or syllables. Not only does such mumbling sound sloppy, but it can make it difficult for listeners to hear what the speaker is saying—especially if the sentence contains a string of words with similar-sounding vowels and consonants. The only effective solution is to enunciate last consonant sounds carefully and deliberately, as distinctly as you can, even if you think you are exaggerating to the point of sounding foolish. Rest assured that it will not sound foolish or exaggerated to your listeners in the church or hall.

Inflection: The human voice has the ability to give the same words dozens of meanings, without the use of additional adjectives or adverbs or explanations. That property is called *inflection*—the ability of the voice to emphasize, accent, or "attack" specific words. The emphasis you place on a word can give a whole new meaning to the overall idea, without the need for a long string of adjectives and adverbs or drawn-out, detailed explanations.

For example, "listen" to the sentence, "I never said he stole money." This sentence can have six different meanings, depending on which of the six words you emphasize. Try it. Repeat this sentence six times, emphasizing a different word each time. Hear the various meanings coming from the same order of words? Even simple words like *yes, no,* and *please* can be given entirely new and different meanings depending on how you emphasize the word.

Pitch: Another property that can enhance the meaning of your words is *pitch,* the highness and lowness of your voice. The sounds every voice makes correspond to the high and low notes on the musical scale. In everyday conversation, you might use only a few notes, but effective speakers/homilists know how to change and vary the pitch of their voices to emphasize key words and ideas. Generally speaking, a higher pitch indicates excitement or urgency, while a lower pitch creates a sense of solemnity or seriousness. Higher-pitched voices tend to carry better than lower-pitched voices; lower-pitched voices can easily become muffled, throaty, or breathy and, consequently, be more difficult to hear and understand. Voices that are too high in pitch, however, are grating to the listener (the "screeching chalk on the blackboard" effect). Just about every speaker can adjust the pitch of his/her voice; a speaker with a naturally high-pitched voice can, with effort and practice, lower the pitch of his/her voice.

Rate: The human voice also has the ability to vary its rate. A quicker rate of speaking can indicate excitement, urgency, or enthusiasm, while a slower rate not only adds emphasis but makes the details of an important point easier for the audience to grasp and follow. Few homilists and public speakers speak too slowly; most speak too fast. A homilist whose delivery seems too slow often has another problem, such as a monotone voice so devoid of variations in pitch and inflection that the community quickly loses interest in what he/she is saying.

Silence: A wise music teacher told his students that anyone can learn the mechanics of playing the piano, that hitting a certain key on the piano will make the sound that corresponds to a certain note on the staff. "Ah, but for a real musician," he said, "the music is not in the notes but in the *pause* between the notes."

Anyone can say or read your notes or text, but the impact, the emphasis, and the insight of the message are made most effectively in the *pause* between the words and ideas. Parents of small children know that if they feed their baby spoonful after spoonful of pablum without stopping, the child will soon be wearing more food than he/she is eating; after awhile, the child may actually fight off the spoonfuls. A similar effect occurs when a presenter allows the fear of silence to result in force-feeding too many ideas, one after another, without letup. The result is the audience suffers "information overload."

Well-timed pauses in a speech can be powerful and effective devices more eloquent and meaningful than words. A well-timed pause gives the listeners time to "absorb" what you have just said, giving them the opportunity to create their own images to accompany your words, thereby increasing retention (and preventing information overload). Stopping for a moment commands attention to what you have said or are about to say. In relating a story or before making a key point, for example, a strategically placed pause creates the element of suspense.

Pausing also works to the speaker's advantage: Stopping helps you eliminate "non-words" and nervous distractions. Inexperienced speakers believe that they have to keep the show moving, so they fill what would otherwise be empty air with annoying non-words like "um," "er," and meaningless verbiage like "okay" and "really." When your mind goes blank, it is better to turn off the sound and get your bearings rather than to ramble on incoherently.

A well-timed and rehearsed pause allows for the special timing needed to emphasize the punch line of a joke or story. Pausing gives you the chance to breathe—to relax and maintain the energy to project and sustain voice quality.

In everyday conversation, we pause naturally because we can sense whether or not our words have been understood by the listener. By reading the faces of our listeners, we know instantly whether or not we are connecting with them; we instinctively stop to make sure the idea has been grasped. For this same reason, it is a good practice to pause for a moment or two at the end of the homily to let the people in the congregation reflect on what they have just heard. (Pausing for a few moments of reflective silence is also suggested after each Scripture reading and after the distribution and reception of communion.)

All of these vocal devices can be effective tools in communicating the homily—but only if you practice using them. More on that follows.

Body Language: The Eyes and the Face

Think about the person you most recently spoke with. Think about that person's face, posture, and hands as the two of you were talking. Didn't they say as much about what that person was feeling and thinking as the words he/she used? It's natural. In one-on-one conversations, our bodies go on a sort of "automatic pilot": Our eyes, face, and hands automatically (naturally) make the "right" gestures and movements—the body is in sync with the words. Effective public speakers have their body in sync with the words of their speech.

Psychologists have found that the eyes and the face account for more than half the emotional impact of a speaker's message. The eyes, for example, can create a bond between the speaker and the listener; *direct eye contact* in particular is perceived as sincere, earnest, forthright, and confident. Due primarily to television, all audiences have come to expect direct eye contact from every speaker, whether priest or politician.

Eye contact begins by seeing your congregation/audience not as some amorphous mass of humanity but as individual human beings. Good eye contact is developed in three stages:

- first, learning to look directly at members of the audience, not staring off over their heads;

- second, learning to see individuals in the audience and noticing things like what audience members are wearing (bright sweaters, glasses), what they are doing (taking notes, nodding off);

- third, reading the audience—being aware of smiles, frowns, approval, puzzlement, etc., that indicate the impact your homily is having.

Many inexperienced homilists and speakers are too willing to sacrifice eye contact for the "smooth" recitation of their words. They believe that reading the text of their presentation, word for word, is better than stumbling and tripping over their words. Don't fall into that trap. Most audiences will gladly tolerate a few "ums" and "ahs" and jerky starts and stops to check notes if they sense that the speaker/homilist is trying to connect with them, that the homilist is attempting to talk to them and not "at" them. That bond is made, first, in one's eye contact with the audience.

The *ready smile* is another important tool in preaching. Walk into a room full of people, especially people you do not know. Who are the individuals you find yourself gravitating toward? Those who smile. A smile is the major bridge-builder in communications. A smile allays fears, invites and welcomes others to come on over, and establishes bonds of friendship and trust. Even the most solemn of liturgies is not undermined by a smile of welcome and invitation. Like the concept of invitation in the preaching model, smiling is as much an attitude, a way of thinking, as it is a physical expression.

Body Language: Gestures and Posture

Say, "This is very important!" with your hands hanging motionless at your sides.

Now say, "This is very important!" shaking your fist as you say the word *very*.

That simple gesture of shaking your first automatically compelled you to say the word *very* with more vigor and force. Effective speakers know how to incorporate gestures to make their points stronger and more memorable.

There are several kinds of *gestures*:

- *conventional gestures:* These are signs and symbols that everyone understands, such as numbers or a raised palm indicating "stop!"

- *descriptive gestures:* These gestures indicate size, direction, or panorama. Some verbs can be described in gestures:

Washing, for example, can be indicated with the hand wiping clean an imaginary blackboard.

- *indicators:* These are gestures used to punctuate or emphasize ideas, such as a clenched fist for anger or solidarity, cupped or clasped hands symbolizing community or completeness, an extended hand inviting the audience to join an effort.

Gestures work, however, only when they are natural. The key is to be relaxed and comfortable, letting the gestures happen. Gestures do not work if they are forced (phony, larger-than-life, or out of sync with the words) or "wishy-washy" (like a weak handshake that conveys fear and indecision).

Posture and *movement* are also critical communications elements in a speech. Good posture projects authority and integrity, and reinforces your enthusiasm in your topic and in the audience. Maintaining good posture is simple: Just keep both feet flat on the floor. Standing stiffly and motionless when addressing the congregation is not natural. Speakers who stand ramrod straight, regardless of the words uttered, communicate, "This is a very formal occasion" or "I am scared to death of all of you" or "I am vastly superior to all of you." Speakers who are careless in maintaining their posture (slumping over or leaning on the podium, for example) tell the audience, "I really don't want to do this" or "I'm too 'cool' to be here" or "Speaking to you now is a waste of my time." Speakers who stand straight, leaning forward a little toward the audience, communicate clearly but silently, "I'm glad I'm here" or "I'm interested in you" or "I want to share something important with you that you'll be glad you had a chance to hear."

Animated movement is one thing but nervous twitching, pacing, and shaking—or what an audience perceives as such—are entirely different. What the speaker might intend as enthusiastic animation might be perceived as nervous energy that makes everyone in the audience uneasy; what the speaker may think is a cool, professional exterior may, in fact, be read by the audience as aloofness and cold dispassion toward the subject and/or the congregation, or simply annoying and distracting. When is something distracting? When the audience starts wondering or whispering, "I wish he'd stop wiggling" instead of "I understand that insight into John's Gospel."

So, when you arrive at the place from where you will speak, plant both feet firmly on the floor so you will not sway back and forth. Remember that the lectern is there not as a defense mechanism or to serve as a brace to hold you up; the lectern is a piece of furniture designed for function, the function of holding the notes and materials you need for your homily.

With the technology of wireless microphones, homilists/speakers are no longer confined to the locus of the lectern, however. Well-timed and well-rehearsed movement helps keep the presentation natural and conversational. It can also project that critical sense of invitation to the audience in the ideas you are presenting. For such movement to work, it must be natural and effortless; any awkwardness and fear will be perceived negatively by the audience.

Again, the key is for all body movement to be relaxed and natural. If you don't use your hands, for example, in everyday conversation, then you will not be able to use them effectively in public speaking. Body movement and gesturing cannot be forced; but the more you become comfortable at the lectern, the more you will develop the confidence to let your body become a natural part of your preaching/presenting.

Preparing Yourself to Preach

In preaching, as in all public speaking, the words (text) are *not* the communications channel; rather, the homilist is the channel or vehicle that delivers the message to the audience. Just as reading the script of a play is a poor substitute for actually seeing and hearing the play performed, it is the homilist's delivery that makes the words come alive for his/her hearers.

The speaker's voice and body communicate as much as his/her words.

Effectively communicating with both verbal and nonverbal elements takes practice. The late actor Robert Preston always posted a small sign in his dressing room: "Security is knowing all your lines." The operative word here is *knowing* your homily—knowing it so that it is *your* message: The words and images are *yours*, you are in *control* of your message, the phrasing is *natural* and *comfortable* to you, you can deliver this speech with natural *enthusiasm*.

The goal of rehearsing is *not* to read or recite (memorize) your homily, however. Today's audiences do not respond to mechanical or impersonal presentations. Thanks again to television, audiences today expect speakers to talk with them in a natural, easy, conversational manner. So once you have the words of your homily on paper, you are halfway there. Next you have to get yourself ready to preach your words.

Words on paper may be effective when a reader reads them off the page. But more often than not, those same words are not as clearly understood or as easily followed when they become spoken words heard by listeners. The words may not roll off the tongue as easily as the writer imagined, and merely "reading" the words squanders the opportunity for the voice and body to bring the words to life.

Wise homilists—preachers who truly want to connect with their audience—will never preach a sermon until they spend time rehearsing it. Here's a method that many professional speakers follow in rehearsing a presentation:

Work with a complete outline, not a full text. With the full text in front of you, you may easily fall into the "reading" mode, thus short-circuiting the eye contact your audience expects from you and the vocal variations and gestures that give life and color to your homily. It is painfully obvious to an audience when a homilist who has been speaking to them in a conversational style suddenly begins to read the text; the homilist's head starts to bob up and down in a noticeable and obtrusive rhythm, looking from the text, to the audience, back to the text, and back to the audience; the homilist's vocal pattern becomes monotonously steady and constant, and variations in pitch and inflection disappear.

One way to generate your outline is to edit your text into "sense" lines. Take a look at the sample homilies at the end of each chapter of this book, and note how each line of text ends at a natural break—the end of a sentence, the end of an idea, or the end of an explanation. Practicing with a text written in "sense" lines helps you get a sense of the rhythm and flow of the text. It also helps you develop effective eye contact, as you look up at the end of that critical word or phrase that will be found at the end of each printed line.

Practice giving the homily OUT LOUD. Going over your homily "in your head" accomplishes little. You have to make your brain and voice work together to bring your homily to life. Rehearse the homily out loud as many times as it takes to get it down—especially the story, the transitions from point to point, and the closing invitation. You will realize immediately those words that look terrific on paper do not "sound" so terrific when verbalized; out loud, you can "find" other words that work more naturally for you. You will realize immediately what words need to be emphasized through voice variation; the places where you should slow down and pause will be readily apparent as well. You also will find places that need editing. You will discover how to improve the flow and rhythm of the presentation, and you will get a sense of timing, of where you should pause, of which words need to be hit harder or softer or slower.

Rehearse your homily out loud several times, across the span of two or three days, if you can.

Practice giving your homily OUT LOUD without your outline. Sure, you're going to stumble, lose your place, forget what comes next. But this exercise will help you learn the flow of the homily and identify where the difficult transitions are. Only then will the homily become yours; only then will you be able to preach it effectively. Your notes should not be a crutch but a safety net to keep you on track. The more you come to know your material, the more command you will have of it, the more poise and confidence you will possess as you preach it, and the more natural your gestures and physical punctuations will be.

Putting the time and care into the physical preparation of the homily is an indispensable factor in communicating a homily that invites people to embrace the love of God.

Some other suggestions for rehearsing your homily:

Practice your homily in the place where you will be speaking. This is especially important if you have never preached in that church before. Get used to the lectern, the lighting, and the acoustics.

"Road test" your homily. Preach your homily to another person or persons if at all possible. Some priests meet weekly to bounce homilies and sermon ideas off one another. Such feedback is indispensable.

For many speakers, practicing with a tape recorder is very helpful. Playing back your practice sessions can help you "hear" the homily as others will hear it on Sunday. Recording your homily as you give it each Sunday—if you can do so quietly and unobtrusively—can be a powerful (and unmerciful) learning tool.

Practice in whatever ways are helpful to you. Some speech coaches urge practicing in front of a mirror, for example; others believe this is a waste of time. "Unless you are going to speak in front of a hundred people who look exactly like you, I don't think its very helpful," one college instructor tells his students.

Dealing with Nervousness

Many homilists/speakers experience some form of nervousness before a presentation—and that's all right. Nervousness, in fact, is a positive sensation that prevents homilists from oversimplifying the task and serves as a control mechanism that prevents them from doing or saying something "ill advised." Anxiety, if channeled creatively, can give you extra energy for the presentation and put a certain luster in your voice that might not otherwise be there if you are too at ease.

Why do people become nervous? There are basically two reasons. The speaker may not be prepared (and if that's the case, the homilist deserves to suffer). The other reason for nervousness is a variation on the complex that the prophet Amos suffered: "I'm no speaker. I'm just a dresser of sycamores" (Amos 7:14). If this is the source of your nervousness, remember three things:

1. You are not vying for an Academy Award here. You are sharing your faith, the most valuable and precious thing you possess, with people you care about and who care about you.

2. You are not Peter on the day of Pentecost, nor Paul at his fiery best. You are here to help these people "make the connections between the realities of their lives and the Gospel." Mass conversions are not your goal; rather, you are helping people discover the presence of God in their lives.

3. This is God's Word you are sharing, not yours. As a homilist, you have been called to serve the people of God. This exercise is not about you. Think about your community first, and your own fears will take care of themselves.

Nervousness is a physical as well as a mental (or spiritual) phenomenon. Notice that when you are nervous, your pulse rate increases significantly. With the blood surging through your body, your breathing becomes quick and short. So when you are nervous, take a deep breath, not from the upper ribs but from the "gut"—that is, from the diaphragm, the large muscle that moves up and down between the abdominal and thoracic cavities.

Try this deep breathing technique the next time you feel tense over your homily. Exhale all the air out of your lungs so that your shoulders shrug. Then inhale, deeply and slowly, and let it our again, slowly. Take a few long breaths and then try to project your voice clearly and loudly. You will find that you have greater voice control and power. You may still be anxious, but you should have a new sense of energy and dynamism in your voice that will give you the confidence to go out there and "give 'em heaven."

Homily #1: Playing Santa

The homilies that follow illustrate various dynamics of *invitation*. The first homily was preached on the Second Sunday of Advent, when John the Baptizer makes his annual appearance in the desert of Judea proclaiming his message of repentance and conversion in preparation for the coming of the Messiah. The pre-Christmas hoopla that upstages the profound message of Advent can be an inviting and easy target for any preacher. The preacher of the following homily takes aim, not with scorn and indignation, but with kindness and insight. The true *story* he relates transforms the Santa Claus myth from the "give me" mentality, that is the antithesis of Christmas, into the "giving" model of discipleship.

A chronically ill toddler
could not always go along with her brother and sister
on their various adventures.
But at Christmastime, Mom and Dad assured her
that she would get to meet Santa Claus.
For weeks the little girl spoke of nothing
but her coming visit to Santa;
Mom prayed for a Santa
who would live up to her daughter's expectations.

Finally, on one of the sick little girl's better days,
Mom decided that this was it.
In order to avoid lengthy lines,
they arrived just as the mall was opening
and Santa was settling into his big chair
　　for the day's onslaught of children.

When the little girl saw him,
she squealed, "Santa Claus!"
and darted past a few assistant elves toward Santa.
The slightly startled Santa
greeted her with a big smile
and swept her into his ample lap.
She snuggled in, stroked his beard,
and uttered in joyful awe, "Santa!"
For several minutes,
Santa and the little girl talked and laughed
like two old friends,
oblivious to the small crowd gathering around
to share in the magic of the moment.

The toddler's mother stood nearby,
her eyes filled with tears of joy.
Just then, a man edged over to her
and, to her surprise,
she noticed that his eyes were as moist as hers.
 "Is that your little girl?" he asked quietly.
The woman nodded.
With a catch in his voice and quiet pride, the man said,
 "Santa is my son."[5]

In his *connection* of this story to the Advent Gospel, the homilist seeks to change our perspective on old Saint Nick.

The proud dad's son is the real Santa Claus—
not the jolly old elf who dispenses toys
to good little girls and boys,
but Nicholas the saint,
the pastor of a small Christian church
    in what is now Turkey,
who was revered
    for his Christ-like kindness and selflessness.
Christmas calls us not to anticipate Santa

but to *become* Santa,
to bring the joy and hope of this season
into the lives of everyone.
Taking on the role of Santa
is not confined to this season alone
but to every season of every year.

To play Santa as the mall Santa in the story
is to become a prophet and messenger of Christ—
a messenger like John the Baptizer,
bearing witness to God's presence among us;
to play Santa in the spirit of the real Saint Nicholas
is to respond faithfully to our baptismal call
to become disciples of the risen Jesus,
to love, to heal, to forgive as he taught.

The homilist concludes by *inviting* his hearers to "become Santa":

Christmas is the season of dreams coming true:
This year become someone's Santa,
making that person's dreams come true.
It is the season of good will to all:
Continue the work of the real "Saint Nick,"
living your call to be disciples of Jesus.
It is the season of peace on earth:
Let your Santa-work this Christmas
take up the cry of John the Baptizer:
The Messiah has come!

Homily #2: The woman who hid Anne Frank

The themes of selflessness and humility preached by Jesus strike at the nerve center of our preoccupation with self, with our culture's obsession with winning at all costs, and with power-everything. It is a tough message that can be tough to hear. Ask those who first heard Jesus' words about following the teachings of the scribes and Pharisees but not imitating their lifestyle (Matthew 23:1–12). A homilist preaching on this Gospel told his community the story of a real woman whose humility became her glory:

> She was not a general.
> She led no troops into battle.
> She was far, far away
> from the centers of political power and military strategy.

> Yet, while she bristles at the term,
> she is one of the true heroes of World War II.

> Fifty years ago,
> this small, quiet woman with white hair,
> with the tentative step
> and the kindly demeanor of a grandmother,
> stood up against and beat
> one of the most sinister manifestations of evil
> human history has ever known.

> Her name is Miep Gies.
> In 1933, she was hired as a secretary
> to a Jewish spice merchant in Amsterdam.
> In 1942, the merchant's oldest daughter was ordered
> by the Nazi occupiers
> to report to a work camp.
> Rather than surrender their lives,
> the merchant and his family placed their fate
> in the hands of the secretary,
> who hid them in the unused annex
>   above the spice warehouse.
> Being a Christian,
> Mrs. Gies was never in the same immediate danger
> as her Jewish friends were.

Hiding them could cost her and her husband their lives.
But for two years,
Mrs. Gies and her husband
provided food, clothing, medical supplies,
and much needed friendship to the family.
The incredible story of the Gies's bravery
was chronicled by the family's younger daughter
in a journal found only later,
after the family was deported:
The Diary of Anne Frank.

Today, the 87-year-old Miep Gies travels around the world
telling her inspiring story.

"I am just a very common person," she tells her audiences.
"I simply had no choice.
I could foresee many sleepless nights,
and a life filled with regret,
if I had refused to help the Franks.
In my opinion,
remorse can be worse than losing your life."

But weren't you afraid? she is always asked.

"This question always surprises me
because I could not think of doing anything else.
Yes, it takes courage,
some dignity, and also some sacrifice
to do your human duty.
But that is true of so many things in life."[6]

The homilist then places Mrs. Gies's *story* in the context of
the Gospel reading (the *connection*):

It is often said that these times
are desperately looking for heroes;

today's Gospel, however, questions where we look for them.
Most heroes are ordinary people who,
when placed in extraordinary situations,
respond with extraordinary courage,
conviction, and perseverance.

There are heroes among us now—
men and women, teenagers and children,
who, in their often unnoticed service to all of us,
stand up to the evils of ignorance,
racism, intolerance, and hatred.
In the power and authority of their actions,
they share with us their vision of faith,
a faith centered in the example of Christ,
the humble servant of God.

But can ordinary folks be Miep Gies? You bet they—and
we—can, concludes the homilist, who ends by *inviting* his hearers to embrace the same spirit of humility as the Gieses:

While we do not face the same danger
that Miep Gies faced in 1942,
our world—
even our own little piece of the world here—
is still plagued by injustice, intolerance, hatred.

Our time, like Miep Gies's time,
cries out for heroes:
men and women of committed faith,
faith that is not expressed in where we sit in church
or the medals and crosses we wear around our necks,
but in the hope we live
and the charity we extend to others.
And such faith begins with humility—
realizing that all we are,
all we have,

is gift from God—
a God whose only motivation in creating us is love.
Miep Gies understood that,
and she was able to do extraordinary, heroic things—
even defying and beating the Third Reich.

Homily #3: Parents know

Homilists who understand the importance of the *invitation* dimension of preaching work hard in their presentation of the homily. Once they have devised the words of their homily, they devote as much time preparing themselves—their voices, their hands, their bodies, their spirits—to preach this homily.

The following homily was preached on the Second Sunday of Lent: the story of that incredible vision that Peter, James, and John witnessed on the mount of the transfiguration. For this homily to be effective, each image must be presented slowly and clearly, and each idea must be articulated with understanding and insight. To accomplish that, the voice and body language of the homilist must be fully engaged in its delivery.

Try reading the following out loud a few times. Each time you read it, let your gestures and vocal intonations become more involved in the delivery. You will quickly see how both the rhythm and flow of these images and words and the rhetorical devices of repetition and parallel construction work to make these images come alive for the hearer.

The *story:*

Ask any parent.
They know.
That the joy of awaiting the birth of a child
soon gives way to the anxiety and pain of labor;
that the happiness and satisfaction that parenthood brings
demands many sleepless nights and worrisome hours.
Parents know.

That, before the triumph
of gliding through the air on a two-wheeler,
scraped knees and banged-up arms will be suffered first;
that before the first victory
on the basketball court or soccer field
comes many hours of hard practices,
the embarrassment of botching up plays,
the humiliation of tough losses;
that before the degree is awarded
there are classes to be attended,
texts and lab experiments to navigate through,
term papers to be written,
projects to be completed,
exams to be passed;
that to get your first job
there are resumes to be worked up and mailed out
and the tedious rounds
of first and second and third interviews to be endured.
Parents know.

That before you find the man or woman of your dreams,
there will be a few nightmares;
that there is a great deal
of pain and doubt and heartbreak
on the road to "happily ever after."
Parents know.

That there is a cost to being a person of integrity;
that the values you believe in the core of your being
do not come cheaply;
that there is a price to be paid
for being the kind of person you want to be.
Ask any parent.
Ask your parents.
They know.

The *connection:*

Parents, more than anyone,
understand the Gospel of the transfiguration:
that resurrection is possible only after crucifixion,
that the passover to life begins in pain,
that the entryway to eternal life is death.
The vision Peter, James, and John witness
    on the mountaintop
is a glimpse of the glory that will be Jesus'—
once he completes the journey to Jerusalem
and the events of Holy Week are fulfilled.

The concluding *invitation:*

Parents know.
That despite the obstacles in the road,
we can make our way to God
with the hope of the transfiguration;
that despite the crucifixions we suffer,
Easter will dawn;
that despite the deaths we endure,
resurrection will come.
Parents know.
That's how they got to be parents.

The invitation dynamic of preaching begins in the heart
and mind of the homilist. It is the expression of an attitude of
caring and understanding, the sense of community, the
homilist's disposition of joy and optimism at the core of his/her
being. It is naturally expressed not only in words but in the sub-
tler but no less expressive vehicles of vocal tone, body attitude,
and body language. Invitation cannot be missed by the com-

munity if the homilist truly possesses it; it cannot be manufactured if it does not exist within the preacher.

A theologian and an eight-year-old were asked the same question: "How would you describe heaven?"

The theologian offers this response in his latest text: "Heaven is in itself eschatalogical reality. It is the advent of the finally and wholly Other. Its own definitiveness stems from the definitiveness of God's irrevocable and indivisible love. Its openness vis-à-vis the total eschaton derives from the open history of Christ's body and, therewith, of all creation which is still under construction."

But the eight-year-old believes: "It's a place where animals don't bite."[7]

So the next time you preach, ask yourself: *Which vision of heaven do I want to invite my people to embrace?*

Chapter 5

The Journey to Sunday

I once heard a preacher who sorely tempted me to say
I would go to church no more. . . .
A snow storm was falling around us.
The snow storm was real,
the preacher merely spectral,
and the eye felt that sad contrast in looking at him
and then out of the window behind him
into the beautiful meteor of snow.
He had lived in vain.
He had not one word intimating
that he had laughed or wept,
was married or in love,
had been commended or cheated or chagrined.
If he had ever lived and acted,
we were none the wiser for it. . . .
The true preacher can be known by this,
that he deals out to the people his life—
life passed through the fire of thought.

From the journal of American essayist
and poet (and one-time minister),
Ralph Waldo Emerson

Like the community they are called to serve, preachers are travelers through time. Their lives, as is every life, are journeys to the dwelling place of God and, on their journeys, they experience the same joys and fears, discoveries and doubts, insights and anguish, that everyone else experiences. They are not immune to heartache, disappointment, and stress. As Emerson quite correctly observes, preaching that is sanitized of such experience is empty preaching.

On a practical level, the process of conceiving, writing, and delivering a Sunday homily is more accurately understood as a journey rather than a formula. What follows are some final practical suggestions for homilists to consider along their journey to Sunday. The four stops or "stations" along the way that wise and faithful homilists travel each week are part of the larger pilgrimage traveled every day by every Christian on the lifelong trek to the kingdom of God.

The First Station: The Wilderness

A young student approached his master and asked him what he needed to do to become a teacher of the Scriptures himself. The rabbi asked him, "And what have you done so far?"

"I have gone through the Torah, verse by verse, chapter by chapter," the would-be scholar replied.

"Good," responded the rabbi, "but has the Torah gone through *you?*"

Jesus frequently retreated to the wilderness, to the out-of-the-way place, in order to regroup mentally and spiritually. Homilists who are serious about preaching also need time in the wilderness to let the Gospel "go through" their being.

Each week, you, the homilist, must spend time alone with the Word that will be the center of your homily. This time of prayer and reflection should focus on some basic questions: *What does this Gospel say to me? How does this Gospel touch my life? Does this Gospel disturb me, make me feel uncomfortable?*

Consider using the following approach: First, read the Gospel on which you will preach *at least a week ahead of time*. Then read that Gospel each evening and morning during that week, and let the reading "percolate" within your subconscious. You will be amazed at how that Gospel will resonate through the week, how that Word will reveal itself in the "stories" you encounter during the week.

Renowned preacher Walter J. Burghardt speaks of this station as a time to "mull over" the Scriptures:

> Now mulling can take a week, maybe three or four weeks, until I get an idea that grabs me. So I do it at various times. I do it while walking around. I do it at the beach. In chapel. Fifteen minutes here or there. Sometimes a couple of hours. Until something grabs me. I'm unwilling to preach on a subject I don't care about. The Scripture reading has to suddenly get a hold of me so I say, "All right!" This can take a fair amount of time.[1]

In this "mulling" process, the Gospel reading may trigger a story; at other times, a story, event, or image will come first, opening up in your imagination a new dimension to a particular Gospel account. Keeping a preaching journal or notebook is an excellent way to capture inspiration when it comes.

Winston Churchill often spent many hours and days at this "station," thinking about and preparing his speeches. Churchill said of this time of gathering his thoughts and ideas: "There is in that act of preparation the moment you start caring."[2]

As you spend time "mulling" in the wilderness with the Word of God, as you make your daily trek through the marketplace, there will come a point when you find yourself "caring" about this homily, "caring" about the message you want to share with your worshiping community, "caring" about the justice and faithfulness you do to the Word of God. Until you care, the homily will be a struggle for you. Unless you care, the community will not.

Your wilderness experience should also deal with another, more personal issue: Preaching is a risky proposition. It demands that you experience the same change and growth that you ask of your hearers. Especially in this day and age, all of us want to project that we, indeed, "have our act together." But if we have learned anything from the Christ story, it is that none of us is "together" without him. We are all sinners; we are all in desperate need of redemption. We all, like the apostle Paul, continue to do the things we know we shouldn't do and avoid doing the things we ought to do. That realization, however, does not make it easy for many of us, ordained or not, to give public witness to such helplessness and vulnerability. To be childlike in professing such total dependence on a loving and merciful Father is to risk making a fool of ourselves. Perhaps that's what being a "fool for Christ" means.[3]

The most generous, faithful approach you can take on many Sundays is not to pretend that you have the answers but invite the community to ask the question in the wilderness of their own hearts. To do that demands the spirit of the servant Christ, the integrity and honesty of the faithful prophet. Such preaching is, in the words of Emerson, "life passed through the fire of thought."

The Second Station: The Marketplace

Throughout the Gospels, Jesus travels through the marketplaces and Temple precincts—the places where people gather every day. He meets people where they live and work and play and pray. His language and stories reflect those places. There is nothing of the "ivory tower" of Jesus' preaching; there is nothing lofty or remote about his language. Jesus moves deliberately between the wilderness and the marketplace of his listeners.

The marketplace is where preachers will find the story that will connect with their listeners. The *story/connection/invitation* model challenges homilists to keep their antennae up and feelers out for the unmistakable signs of God's presence in the world they share with their worshiping community. It demands that they be aware of the places in their own lives where they, themselves, have discovered God, the times when God has touched their lives, the many Good Fridays in their lives that God has transformed into Easter mornings. It also demands listening to the "stories" of their worshiping community, listening to their experiences of joy, fulfillment, pain, doubt, anguish, and despair.

Preaching is, in the end, the bringing together of the wilderness and the marketplace. In reflecting on his own preaching, Robert McAfee Brown observed that homilists are called to wrestle with two apparently unlikely realities: the world of Scripture and the world of the here and now:

> No matter where one started, the sermon [is] not a sermon until those two worlds finally came together, each illuminating the other until they could not be separated. Karl Barth's famous aphorism vindicated itself dozens of times: "The Christian must always read the Bible in one hand and the morning paper in the other."[4]

So if preaching is an important part of your ministry, walk with your community in their journeys. Listen rather than judge. Understand before criticizing. Realize that their doubts, fears, and vulnerability are not unlike your own.

Be in touch with the world around you by reading a reliable newspaper every day. Read national magazines like *Newsweek*, *Time* and, yes, *People*. See a popular movie now and then, and check out the books that people are talking about. And don't miss the many wonderful stories that are told on television newsmagazine programs. Where is God found on these pages, in these pictures? How is the Spirit at work in these stories? What is the Jesus of the Gospel speaking in these events?

Remember that preaching is not an academic exercise, not a lecture, and not a detached discourse. Rather, preaching is one pilgrim sharing his/her story with another pilgrim. It is your story of meeting Jesus in the marketplaces you negotiate, of discovering the presence of God in your life.

The Third Station: The Empty Temple

The unforgivable sin in preaching is not being prepared. Most preachers would not think of getting up before the worshiping assembly without taking the time necessary to prepare the words of the homily. But what about *preparing the homilist* for the homily?

To have the words is not enough. In any oral presentation, the real vehicle for communication is not the words but the speaker of those words. It is the speaker's vocal inflection, eye contact, and body attitude that give these words life beyond the letters on the page. To prepare a homily effectively means to prepare the homilist, as well, to deliver that homily.

Before rushing up the steps of the sanctuary to dazzle the people of God, spend some time at the church before the community gathers. Once you have prepared the *story*, *connecting ideas*, and *invitation* of your homily, spend time preparing yourself to tell that *story*, to *connect* that story to the theme of the Gospel, to *invite* your listeners to embrace the love of God that is revealed in that Gospel. The moment you begin your homily before the assembly on Sunday should not be the first time you hear the words coming out of your mouth.

Homilists can learn from the experience of professional speakers like comedian Jay Leno, for example. In interviews with *The New York Times Magazine* and the television newsmagazine *Dateline: NBC*, the host of NBC-TV's *The Tonight Show* discussed the work that goes into writing the jokes for his eleven-minute monologue each night.[5]

The work begins the night before. After devouring several daily newspapers and magazines, Leno and his writers come up with several hundred jokes and one-liners—but only twenty-five will make the final cut. The best jokes, each written on an individual index card, make it to the "A" pile.

Leno will then record on an audio cassette the jokes he particularly likes. From listening to the playback, Leno is able to determine what words to stress and spin and how to time the hesitations that make vocalized comedy so much richer than written words. From his many years working small comedy clubs, Leno has developed a gift for the meter and rhythm of comic cadence; he has learned how to tighten the wording and pacing of his jokes. Leno will record the jokes several more times before he is satisfied with the wording, sequence of jokes, and associations. Many evenings, the comedian will try out his monologue jokes the night before at a small comedy club in Los Angeles. The audience reaction is often the determining factor if a particular joke makes it to the following day's *Tonight Show* taping. As Jay Leno knows all too well, speaking simply and effectively demands a great deal of work; having the words written on cue cards is not enough. To communicate words with sincerity, conviction, and meaning demands a great deal of care and hard work.

The third station is the empty temple where that hard work of preparing yourself to preach the Word takes place. Before the community gathers in the "temple," take the time to put the right words together and to rehearse those words so that you can articulate them with the right emphasis, passion, and humor, to learn the timing and rhythm of those words.

The Fourth Station: The Temple Gates

There is a fourth station still to be marked *after* the homily is given: the temple gates. This station challenges homilists to ask the hard question: *Did the congregation get the intended message of the homily?*

Every professional communicator realizes that the meaning and success of a message are determined not by the sender of the message but by the intended receiver. Good communicators, then, intentionally solicit and consider any feedback from their audience. Homilists who take seriously the preaching ministry will go to the "temple gates" to seek out the reaction of the community. It can be hard to listen to the good and bad of your presentation, but there is no better learning experience.

The "temple gates" station may take the form of inviting a few parishioners to have coffee with you after Mass while you ask them what they heard and thought about the Liturgy of the Word—of which your homily was a part. Especially seek the reactions of lectors, who provide an important service to the community in proclaiming the Word you preached. Some parish liturgy committees organize focus groups and design survey instruments to determine how their communities respond to all the elements of worship, including preaching.

If you are able to record your homilies on Sunday, spend some time listening to them to determine for yourself if they "sounded" as you hoped they would, if your words and images were real, if you were comfortable with your delivery; but do not listen to your homily the same Sunday you preach it—it is far more revealing to hear how it sounds on Monday morning.

Especially if you are a novice homilist, find a mentor whose approach to preaching you appreciate and wish to emulate. Many colleges have communications and speech departments; perhaps one of their faculty would be willing to work with you or a group of clergy from the area.

Remember: Preaching is a form of foot-washing. It is a ministry of love. Like all such ministries, preaching demands the selflessness of the servant Christ in order to place the needs and good of others above oneself. It involves risk. It demands reaching out to take the first and last step in the hard work of helping your hearers realize the presence of God in their lives. To do that with conviction demands a stop at the "temple gates" after the "temple" service.

Homily: *The great Easter wedding feast*

Let's follow one homilist on his journey. The challenge confronting this preacher (as assigned by the pastor and parish worship committee) was to reflect on the liturgies of the Easter Triduum in an attempt to help the community understand and appreciate the annual celebration of the Lord's passion, death, and resurrection as the high point of the Church year. The homily would be preached the week before Palm Sunday. Given the scope of the assignment, the preacher gave himself a little more time than usual to prepare this homily.

The wilderness: The homilist began by reading the three Gospels for the Triduum: John's Last Supper story of Jesus washing his disciples' feet (Holy Thursday), John's account of the passion and death of Jesus (Good Friday), and the resurrection Gospel (the Easter Vigil). He also read through the prayers and rituals of the three Triduum liturgies and made notes on his own memories of the Triduum—of those parts of the liturgies that impress him every year, of his own struggles to enter into the mood and meaning of the liturgy.

The marketplace: As all of these images "percolated" in his consciousness, the preacher continued to make his way every day through the marketplace. He kept his "antenna" tuned to signs of God's presence in the everyday. He kept his ears open to the stories of others discovering, wrestling, and arguing with God in their lives.

At the beginning of his journey, the homilist was overwhelmed by the topic handed to him. This could easily become three homilies, one on each of the three liturgies of the Triduum. With so much to say, so much to share, this homily could quickly become a lecture on liturgy rather than a prayerful reflection.

As he "mulled" it all over, he asked himself what each liturgy "teaches," what Christ is saying to us in the movements of the Triduum that strike us in our everyday lives.

Somewhere between the wilderness and the marketplace, the homilist had a visit from his young nephews—a visit that became the story that centered the homily and helped the homilist sharpen the focus of what he wanted to say.

The empty temple: In the quiet of the "empty temple," the homilist began to pull it all together and, in the course of a couple of days, he wrote out what he wanted to say. He edited the homily several times for overall length (he wanted to keep his homily to no more than twelve minutes), sentence construction, and wording.

Once he had the ideas focused and refined, the homilist gave himself time to work with the text. He reduced the text to a series of notes and then launched into the first of several practice runs. In rehearsing the homily out loud, he quickly discovered the words that sounded false and unreal, the sentences that were too complex to express clearly, and the transition points at which he faltered. He made changes as needed by simplifying and clarifying sentences, and adding and underlining notes and key words. He rehearsed the homily out loud several more times until he was comfortable with the flow of the ideas and the vocal and physical elements of his delivery.

Here is what the homilist shared with his community that Fifth Sunday of Lent. He began with the *story* that helped him center the homily:

When our nephews were visiting not too long ago,
they discovered a book of photographs
    we keep in our living room—our wedding album.
As they started thumbing through the pages,
the questions started:

"How did you meet?
When did you decide to get married?
Who's that in that photograph?"
In answering their questions,
my wife and I found the whole experience
of our meeting at a conference in Los Angeles,
of our falling in love,
of our wedding,
coming alive for us again—
the joys, the excitement, the terror (!)—
of October 9, 1983.

And our nephews were learning
      something about their family—
and, as a consequence, something about themselves.

Stories and memories make us who we are.
We learn from our stories and memories.
We find our identity in our stories and memories.

The stories and memories we share bind us together—
they bind us together as family,
as friends,
as a parish.

Every time we gather together here for Mass,
we come to rehear the story of Jesus,
we come to share the memory of Jesus—
the story and memory that make us the Church.

Next week, Holy Week, we celebrate the story
in which we find our identity as Christians,
the memory that makes us more than just a service club
or an association of basically good people.

The story of the passion, death, and resurrection
    of Jesus Christ
makes us the Church, the people of God.

The amazing thing I have found
    about the Holy Week liturgies
is that, when the Holy Week liturgies are well planned
    and well prayed,
the story lives again,
the memory of Jesus becomes real.

Although Holy Thursday, Good Friday,
    and Holy Saturday
each mark distinct events in the great passion story,
they are really one event—
the *pascha* or passover of Christ.
The Triduum is like a play, with two or three acts—
you don't get the full story without all three acts . . .
or it's like a symphony,
with several distinct movements,
but a single work.

The homilist continued by *connecting* the idea of remem-
bering the story of Jesus to each of the three "movements" of
the Easter symphony:

The first movement, the first act,
is Holy Thursday evening.

The passion story begins with the Last Supper.
We all know the story of Jesus taking bread and wine
and instituting the sacrament we know as the Eucharist.
The Gospels and the apostle Paul all tell that story.

But the Evangelist John focuses his Last Supper story
on something else that happened that night.

We often hear Holy Thursday referred to as
    "Maundy Thursday."
The word *maundy* comes from the Latin word *mandatum*
from which comes our English word *mandate*.
The *mandatum* of Holy Thursday
is the example of Christ
    who washed the feet of his disciples.

It's hard for us to imagine
how shocked the disciples were
to see their revered teacher take off his robe
and perform the degrading and humiliating task
of washing the dusty, dirty feet of the Twelve—
a job that was reserved only for the lowliest slave.
(Peter can't handle it!)

But that is the *mandatum* Christ leaves
to all of us who claim discipleship:
If I washed your feet,
I who am Teacher and Lord,
then you must wash each other's feet . . .
As I have done, you must do.

On Holy Thursday night here at our parish,
the story of the *mandatum* is retold
as the pastor washes the feet of 12 parishioners.

The first time I ever saw the washing of feet,
my right foot was part of the program.
It was in the college church
and the celebrant that night was the dean.
In any college, the dean is *the* authority figure—
yet here he was,
kneeling in front of me,
washing my foot.
It made a powerful impression on me.
I will never forget that story.

The washing of feet serves as a "visual homily"
of Jesus' last will and testament to his Church.
As John's Gospel recalls,
the Eucharist given to us on Holy Thursday
comes with a steep price:
You must love one another as I have loved you—
without conditions, without limits.

The second movement—Good Friday.
Good Friday is the only day in the Church year
when Mass is *not* celebrated.
It is a day of quiet, of austerity.

But we don't mark Good Friday as if we don't know
how the story finally turns out.
We know full well that Good Friday is *not* the end
     of the Jesus story.

But it is a day that confronts us with the fact
that we all have crosses to bear,
that crucifixions take place in our world every day,
that betrayal, injustice, abandonment, rejection, ridicule,
are all part of the human experience.

The liturgy of Good Friday confronts us
with our *need* for Good Friday—
that we are sinners,
that we are capable of inflicting great hurt on one another,
that we yearn for redemption, for making things right.

The broken body of Jesus confronts us
with our own brokenness.

One part of the Good Friday liturgy
is the veneration of the cross—
kissing a piece of wood!

Personally, I've always felt very self-conscious doing it.
Frankly, it's humiliating.
But that act is a powerful statement of our faith in the
Easter promise:
In Christ, the wood of the cross
is the tree of life for us.
Kissing the wood of the cross is a profession of faith:
that we understand the point of the story
God is telling us
in the death of his own Son.

The third and final part of the story—the Easter Vigil.

Maybe it's a symptom of aging,
but I have to tell you that, for me,
Easter Eve is the best night of the year.
It's certainly the holiest night of the year.
Christmas is great, but it's not Easter.

There are so many parts to the Easter Vigil
that I could never do them all justice here.
But the single most important theme
      of the vigil story is *newness*.
From the candles to the eucharistic bread,
from our new Easter outfits
      to the baptism of new Christians,
everything is new.
A new fire illuminates our darkened church.
A new paschal candle is blessed
as a symbol of risen Christ's presence in our midst
every day of every year.

And we hear the story of God's dream
of creating a people to love and to love him.
And that, despite ourselves,
God refuses to give up on his creation—

we hear how, in the resurrection of his Son,
we are re-created—
God's dream of a holy people will not be denied.
The Easter Vigil is the memory of a God
whose love is stubborn and perseverant,
a God who seeks us out when we are lost,
a God who refuses to abandon us in our own darkness,
a God who always invites us to start over
however many times as it takes for us
to we get our story right.

Having started with the memory of a wedding, the homilist
concluded with an *invitation* to a wedding feast:

The pastor asked me to share these reflections with you
as a way of inviting you to participate
in this year's Easter Triduum here at our parish.

The complete schedule of liturgies and services
will be found in next week's parish bulletin.

I began by talking about a wedding.

Throughout Scripture and the Gospels,
God declares again and again
that he loves us with the intimacy and completeness
of beloved spouses—
God loves us as a husband loves his wife,
as a wife loves her husband,
as parents love their children.

In the reading from Isaiah
that we will hear at the Easter Vigil,
the prophet announces:
"He who has become your spouse is your Maker.
The Lord calls you back

like a spouse forsaken and grieving;
My love will never leave you,
nor my covenant of peace be shaken,
says the Lord of mercy."

The Triduum is the great wedding feast of the Risen One.
Come and be part of this year's celebration.
It is a story to celebrate again and again.
It is the memory that makes us who we are.

Let the final word on the homilist's journey belong to novelist and preacher Frederick Buechner:

> If preachers decide to preach about hope, let them preach
> out of what they themselves hope for. . . . And let them
> talk with equal honesty about their own reasons for hoping—not just the official, doctrinal, biblical reasons, but
> the reasons rooted deep in their own day-to-day experience. They have hope that God exists because from time
> to time they have been touched by God. Let them speak
> of those times with candor and concreteness and passion
> without which all the homiletical eloquence and technique in the world are worth little. They believe that
> Jesus is the resurrection and the life because at a few precious moments that is what they have found him to be in
> their own small deaths and resurrections. Let them speak
> of those moments not like essayists or propagandists but
> like human beings speaking their hearts to their dearest
> friends. . . . [6]

God speed on your journey.

Endnotes

Chapter 1: A Gospel Model: "The Reign of God Is Like..."

1. *The Door*, January/February 1996.

2. *For Better or For Worse* by Lynn Johnston, October 26, 1995 (Universal Press Syndicate).

Chapter 2: Story: To "Reveal What Is Hidden"

1. Rabbi Harold S. Kushner. *When Bad Things Happen to Good People* (1981: Avon Books), 110–111.

2. Joseph Bernardin. "Meeting Was Grace-filled: 'We Both Sought Reconciliation'"; *National Catholic Reporter*, January 13, 1995, 20.

3. "Kindest Cut: The Friends of Ian O'Gorman Proved Just How Beautiful Bald Can Be" *People Weekly*, April 11, 1994, 60.

4. Neil Simon. *Broadway Bound*, Act 2.

5. Kathryn Slattery. "Out of Molasses Swamp"; *Guideposts*, September 1986.

6. *Calvin and Hobbes* by Bill Watterston, December 20, 1993 (Universal Press Syndicate).

Chapter 3: Connection: "The Word Made Flesh..."

1. Garry Wills. *Context*, August 15, 1988, volume 20, number 15, 2.

2. Karl-Josef Kuschel. *Laughter: A Theological Reflection* (1994: The Continuum Publishing Company), 104.

3. Charles Osgood. *Osgood on Speaking: How to Think on Your Feet Without Falling on Your Face* (1988: William Morrow and Company), 45.

4. Ron Hoff. *"I Can See You Naked": A Fearless Guide to Making Great Presentations* (1992: Andrews and McMeel), 76.

5. Kathleen Norris. *Amazing Grace: A Vocabulary of Faith* (1998: Riverhead/Penquin Putnam), 187.

Chapter 4: Invitation: "Your Attitude Must Be Christ's"

1. Avery Dulles. *Apologetics and the Biblical Christ* (1963: Paulist-Newman Press), 39.

2. Ron Hoff. *"I Can See You Naked": A Fearless Guide to Making Great Presentations* (1992: Andrews and McMeel), 4.

3. Peggy Noonan. *On Speaking Well* (1998: ReganBooks), 50.

4. Kenneth L. Woodward. "Heard any good sermons lately?" *Newsweek*, March 4, 1996.

5. Ruth Dalton. "Santa Is my Son"; *Reader's Digest*, December 1997.

6. Julie Strauss. "The Woman Who Hid Anne Frank"; *The Diocese of Orange* [California] *Bulletin*, April 1996.

7. Michael J. Farrell. *National Catholic Reporter*, October 4, 1991. Reprinted with permission.

Chapter 5: The Journey to Sunday

1. Walter J. Burghardt. Quoted in "Preaching: blood, sweat and fears," *Modern Liturgy*, September 1988, volume 15, number 7, 11.

2. Peggy Noonan. *On Speaking Well* (1998: ReganBooks), 30.

3. Walter H. Graham. "Practicing the Art of Preaching"; *Church*, Spring 1986, 12.

4. Robert McAfee Brown. "A funny thing happened on the way to the pulpit"; *Christian Century*, July 27–August 3, 1994, 724.

5. Peter Tauber. "Jay Leno: Not Just Another Funny Face"; *The New York Times Magazine*, February 26, 1989; and *Dateline: NBC*, NBC-TV, October 9, 1996.

6. Frederick Buechner. *The Longing for Home: Recollections and Reflections* (1996: HarperSanFrancisco), 172, 173.

Permissions

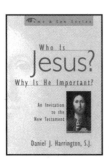
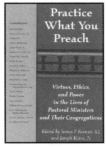
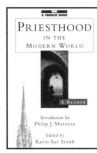
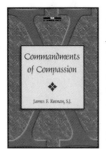